# OVER THE LINE

# AL STRACHAN

Foreword by ROY MacGREGOR

# OVER

*Wrist Shots, Slap Shots,*

# THE

*and Five-Minute Majors*

# LINE

FENN

M&S

Library and Archives Canada Cataloguing in Publication

Strachan, Al
Over the line : wrist shots, slap shots and five-minute majors / Al Strachan.

ISBN 978-0-7710-8341-9

1. National Hockey League – Anecdotes.
2. Hockey – Anecdotes. 3. Strachan, Al. I. Title.

GV847.8.N3S853 2011     796.962'64     C2011-905586-4

We acknowledge the financial support of the Government of Canada through the Book Publishing Industry Development Program and that of the Government of Ontario through the Ontario Media Development Corporation's Ontario Book Initiative. We further acknowledge the support of the Canada Council for the Arts and the Ontario Arts Council for our publishing program.

Published simultaneously in the United States of America by McClelland & Stewart Ltd., P.O. Box 1030, Plattsburgh, New York 12901

Library of Congress Control Number: 2011935491

Typeset in Garamond by M&S, Toronto

Printed and bound in the United States of America

McClelland & Stewart Ltd.
75 Sherbourne Street
Toronto, Ontario
M5A 2P9
www.mcclelland.com

1  2  3  4  5     15  14  13  12  11

This one is for Christie Blatchford who never enters a room as much as she explodes into it. She refers to me as the best husband she never had, and takes great delight in embarrassing me in print. But I've never known anyone as kind.

# CONTENTS

FOREWORD BY ROY MacGREGOR                    ix

INTRODUCTION                                  1
CHAPTER ONE                                   5
CHAPTER TWO                                  19
CHAPTER THREE                               38
CHAPTER FOUR                                56
CHAPTER FIVE                                70
CHAPTER SIX                                 87
CHAPTER SEVEN                              100
CHAPTER EIGHT                              120
CHAPTER NINE                               138
CHAPTER TEN                                149
CHAPTER ELEVEN                             171
CHAPTER TWELVE                             192
CHAPTER THIRTEEN                           209
CHAPTER FOURTEEN                           231
CHAPTER FIFTEEN                            251

ACKNOWLEDGEMENTS                           267

# FOREWORD
## BY ROY MacGREGOR

It is unusual for a book to reduce you to two types of tears, but Al Strachan has managed exactly that with this compelling look at the world of hockey and the world of journalism that covers that magnificent game.

I laughed until I cried at some parts. And I wept for what has become of sports journalism over recent years.

If there is a pendulum swinging in the journalism world that covers hockey, it should, on a perfect day, sit somewhere in the middle, with the breaking news and minutiae – small trades, contractual breakdowns, league suspensions, etc. – on one side and "storytelling" on the other. There has traditionally been these two talents in sports journalism and they both acknowledge, respect, and even need each other. One does the telling; the other the explaining. One introduces; the other gets to know the player, the coach, the owner, the villain (not always to be confused).

In the past several years, there have two critical developments that have skewed hockey journalism. One is the "baseball-ization" of the game – an American-driven need to reduce this game of chance and of creativity to a game of predictions and projections. It began with the National Hockey League issuing game sheets that broke down each match into multiple segments, some of them actually helpful (ice time), some of them debatable (half of faceoffs are neither won nor lost by the ones taking the faceoff), some of them absurd (takeaways and giveaways, which should, in fact, be credited to whichever player created the situation where a puck is gained or lost). So far has this "baseball-ization" gone that there are even complicated formulae developed to prove which players are the most defensively responsible, though the players the numbers claim to honour invariably leave real hockey people scratching their heads in total bafflement. There has never been a formula developed for the single most important criterion in any hockey game: shit happens.

The second critical development has been the Internet. While this has proved a boon to research and even review (journalists sitting in press boxes can cue up a critical replay moments after the play takes place), and while it has allowed thousands a voice that traditional journalism never allowed, it has also been extremely damaging to the concept of what passes for "news" in sport.

Largely because of Twitter, the critical element in hockey journalism today has become "who's first?" Nothing else seems to matter. So important has it become to be seen to be first that the most meaningless minutia – a trade of two players you never heard of in a minor league you've never heard of – gets trumpeted as if it's the Esposito trade to Boston or the Gretzky sale to Los Angeles. Dancing thumbs will even argue over who was first with such a non-story as the impending retirement of Detroit Red Wings Brian Rafalski – an event that in the pre-Twitter days would have amounted to a small uncredited "note" in the sports pages.

This has all managed to turn sports television into a bit of a laugh. During critical moments during the season – trading deadline, impending suspensions, etc. – the multiple talking panels on sports television show little more than men in dark suits fiddling with their BlackBerries as they stare into their tiny screens blissfully unaware of how ludicrous it appears in the big screen. As one very proper English writer once said to me as she happened to catch such a session, "It looks as if they're masturbating."

In many ways they are. What Twitter and blogging has become, in no small part, is public masturbation. Size matters, as in number of followers.

Some will say this is all sour grapes and I would like to smile right back at them and say "Of course it is." Sour because storytelling is largely dead. Sour because the pendulum has swung so far into the muck of minutia that it is stuck. Television is so caught up in this largely meaningless minutia that hardly ever is a compelling story told any longer on television. *Hockey Night In Canada*, which used to do such a splendid job of taking fans inside the lives of players, now rarely bothers even to try, so caught up is the program in its own self-importance. As for TSN and Sportsnet, their best "stories" are, ironically, done in print, on their websites, the television reserved almost exclusively for panels that are growing just a tad . . . tired, shall we say. There is some good analytical work done there by some of the best minds in the game, but not nearly enough stories told.

There is another issue, far more difficult to address. And that is the effect over the control of the supply of information. So much of what has become deemed important in hockey these days comes only via the National Hockey League – information on contracts, trades, suspensions, ownership, rule changes – that it has made those who deal in such information, whether they fully realize this or not, beholden to the National Hockey League. There is such precious little objective criticism of the league that those watching and listening cannot but wonder if the control of minutia has more than somewhat become the control of thought.

There is nothing wrong with having and cultivating sources. We all do. We all need to. But there needs to be a fix. If those panels were balanced out with additional members who are not beholden to the NHL tap of information, but who instead have and express their own thoughts on the game and where it should be going, the sports channels and hockey fans would benefit hugely. As the situation is today structured, balance is impossible.

Al Strachan and I have always enjoyed the fact that we agree on so little – he thinks Attila the Hun was soft, I think Gandhi was harsh – but we certainly agree on the death of storytelling in hockey journalism. And that is why this book is not only so terrific to read but is a truly welcome wake-up call to those of us working in the trade. Al tells stories as well as anyone the business has ever known. You want to know about Eddie Shore's attitude toward goaltending, about luggage on an NHL team, about curfews, wooden sticks, playoff beards . . . listen to Al. You want to understand the business of hockey, read Al on Jim Balsillie. You want to know the inside story on how coach Pat Burns was denied the Hockey Hall of Fame as he lay on his death bed, read Al Strachan and be prepared to weep.

This is storytelling. It is storytelling by one of the most literate, smart, and funny people the game has ever know. It's a treasure. It's the national game as we used to know and – the swinging pendulum willing – we should once again return to. A balance is terribly needed, and with luck the first small push back from the trap of minutia will begin in these pages.

Roy MacGregor

# INTRODUCTION

*The other thing about journalism is that although at the top end it seems to attract well educated, even intelligent, people, it's basically quite unbelievably easy. You ask a question and you write down the answer. You repeat the process a few times. Then you see what all the answers add up to, put them in sequential order with a simple linking narrative and go to the pub.*

Sebastian Faulks, *Engleby*

**During the 2004 World Cup of Hockey**, I spent every day with Team Canada – from the first day of training camp to the night they hoisted the trophy. The tournament ran for about four weeks, and during that time, I talked to almost everyone involved with Team Canada – the players, the coaches, the broadcasters – and even a few agents who dropped in to check out the developments.

I was in the process of retiring, and I was trying to figure out where to do it. What better group to ask than a few dozen millionaire Canadians with real-estate knowledge from coast to coast? I won't go into all the observations that

1

were offered, but the eventual conclusion was that the best place in Canada to settle down was somewhere along the shores of the Bay of Fundy. In that area, we could be assured of friendly people, clean air, good quality of life, cheap property that had a reasonable chance of appreciation, and coastal living.

Within days of the tournament ending, I had bought a house in St. Andrews, New Brunswick, a beautiful little town that offers all the attributes listed above, and started cutting back on work, a process that was hastened when I wrote *Why the Leafs Suck* and was fired from *Hockey Night in Canada* as a result.

It didn't really matter. I was glad to be retired.

But then I was asked if I would write a book sharing some of my memories of four decades in hockey. Since I've repeatedly tried to get Scott Bowman to tell a few stories about the inner workings of the game – stories that would be much more insightful than mine – I could hardly refuse when I was asked. Then it happened again. I was asked to write another.

So much for retirement.

Still, it's not a bad thing to pass along some of these stories and to offer my opinion on a few matters affecting hockey.

One more thing: While I was travelling with hockey teams, I invariably carried a book. When I came across a quote that jumped off the page, I'd write it down. Some of those memorable quotes got lost along the way. Some of the ones I managed to keep will appear at the beginning of each chapter. Don't expect them to necessarily relate to what follows them. They might. They might not. I just thought they were good quotes, and they deserved to be shared.

# CHAPTER ONE

*Publication is a powerful thing. It can bring a man all manner of unlooked-for events, making friends and enemies of perfect strangers, and much more besides.*

Matthew Kneale, *English Passengers*

**It is almost inaccurate** to say that I started covering hockey in 1973. The game that I wrote about in that year bears no resemblance to the game called hockey in 2011.

Here are twenty quick facts about hockey in 1973 that are not true about hockey in 2011:

1. All sticks were made of wood.
2. Helmets were optional and rare. There was even a goalie – Andy Brown of the Pittsburgh Penguins – who played without a mask.
3. All two-line passes were illegal.
4. There was no advertising on the rink boards or on the ice surface.
5. Most teams were coached by one man with no assistants.

6. The crease was rectangular.
7. Bench-clearing brawls were commonplace.
8. Players wore tube skates.
9. Teams were not allowed to call time out.
10. There were sixteen teams in the National Hockey League.
11. There was no instigator rule.
12. There were no European players in the league.
13. Overtime did not exist during the regular season.
14. Shootouts did not exist.
15. There was no video replay.
16. Most games were not televised.
17. The goaltender could play the puck anywhere in his half of the rink.
18. Players' pads were soft.
19. The Stanley Cup was always awarded in early May. In 1973, the ceremony took place on May 10.
20. The game was officiated by one referee, not two.

Those are just some of the tangible differences that are obvious to anyone who has been watching throughout the last four decades, even to those who do not understand the nuances of hockey.

There are many others. And there are also many more subtle changes that have significantly affected the way the game is played today.

In 1973, a winger skated up and down his wing. Because the NHL had been exposed to Soviet hockey only a year earlier, during the Summit Series, there was no European influence. There was none of the swirling, wide-open game that every team plays today. And while those wingers were dutifully skating up and down their wings, they were often checking their opposite number, who just as dutifully stayed on his wing. The checking, such as it was, was implemented by skating alongside the opponent.

Today, wingers and centres skate backwards to do much of their checking. A player breaking out of his own end can look up and see six opponents facing him. That would never have happened in 1973.

If a more physical approach were required, you would bump your opponent into the boards. Although there was the occasional exception, it's safe to say that for the most part, you bodychecked a player in an attempt to get the puck.

Today, you bodycheck him to take him out of the play. It's called finishing the check, and it's all but mandatory.

The concept was initiated by Mike Keenan, who wanted to make opponents leery of being in possession of the puck. In theory, they'd get rid of the puck as soon as possible, even if it was dangerous to do so, and their timidity would give Keenan's boys an opportunity to capitalize.

The problem is that the practice of finishing the check has become so widespread that it has resulted in a host of players who don't really care whether there's a puck on the ice. They just want to go out and finish their checks.

When a scoring chance developed in 1973, the shooter looked for an open area of the net and aimed for it. Today, as often as not, there is no open area of the net to see.

The goalies have mountains of padding, and their skating ability is so vastly superior to that of their 1973 counterparts that they can come out and cut the angle without worrying that they'll be trapped.

You didn't have to shoot high to score in 1973. When I once goaded Ken Dryden by announcing that the scouting report on him said he could be beaten by low, hard shots to the stick side, he responded with a sigh and a statement that was perfectly true in those days: "Al, *every* goalie can be beaten by low, hard shots to the stick side."

Today, goalies drop into the butterfly position at the first hint of a shot and thereby cover the lower fourteen inches of the net. Low, hard shots to the stick side rarely go in.

There were no butterfly goalies in 1973. Far from it. The legendary coach Eddie Shore insisted that his goalies remain standing. He was so adamant on this point that in practice, he was known to tie one end of a rope to his goalie's neck and the other end to the crossbar. Shore was involved in hockey until 1976, and even though he was no longer coaching, his approach to the game was widely followed.

The players' regimen in 1973 was totally different as well. Training camp lived up to its name. It was for training. Players relaxed all summer or "worked" for beer companies – often by playing softball at a brewery-sponsored event. When they came to camp, they did so to lose excess weight (if you're playing beer-league softball, you don't drink milk after the game) and to get in shape for the coming season.

A common refrain from coaches in the early part of the seventy-eight-game season used to be, "We're not in shape yet."

You never hear that any more. Players today do not get out of shape. They might cut down their workout load for two or three weeks, but by August, they're back in the rink, getting ready for the upcoming eighty-two-game season. They also have team trainers and personal trainers.

The 1973 trainer carried equipment bags, sharpened skates, and kept the stick rack full.

Today's trainer is qualified to make a number of medical decisions and is an integral part of the players' conditioning. After games, he or the team masseur – another position that did not exist in 1973 – can work on players while they're on their charter flights.

In 1973, a team might have had a charter during the playoffs, but the rest of the time, it travelled on commercial flights the morning after the game.

Today, visiting teams are usually on the way to the airport forty-five minutes after the game. At the time of day when the 1973 team would have been on the bus to the airport, still in the city where it had played the previous night, today's team is getting up for breakfast in the destination city or at home.

For the most part, these changes in the game have to be seen as improvements. The 2011 game is not perfect. Nothing ever is. But it's fast, physical, and intense.

Also, thanks to Colin Campbell, the skilled players now have a chance to exhibit those remarkable skills. When Campbell took over from Brian Burke as the NHL vice-president responsible for the on-ice spectacle, the game was more like rugby than hockey. The clutchers and grabbers were relentless, and the league suffered from Formula 1 syndrome. Once you got in front, you stayed there.

That's no longer the case. Even three-goal leads are not safe today, and as a result, fan interest is maintained.

But there is one drawback to today's game. When I started covering hockey, the dressing room was a place that lived up to its name. That's where the players dressed. You went in there after a game to talk to the players – and they were there. If they weren't, you could wait them out. Unless they wanted to go home naked or in their hockey gear, they were going to come into that room at some point. It's where their clothes were.

But in the late seventies, certain areas became off limits. The training room had always been that way. That was fine. It was where the players were treated for injuries, and it was tiny anyway – with room for little more than a bed and a few cupboards.

But then came a weight room that was off limits. Then there were players' lounges that were off limits. Now there are always two dressing rooms – one where the players come out to meet the media, should the mood strike, and one where they actually get dressed.

The presence of female reporters provides a handy rationalization for this development, but the move to back rooms was under way before women started going into the dressing rooms. Furthermore, because the players are in a rush to get on the charter flight and get out of town, the media don't get a chance to go out afterwards to share a beer with a few of them and pick up some entertaining not-for-attribution anecdotes. That used to be a staple of the job.

I have said many times that hockey players are the most accessible, articulate, and interesting athletes in any sport anywhere. The changes that have impacted the game have made them less accessible, but that's not their fault. They're still entertaining and interesting.

• • •

But that's the modern era. Not long ago, it was important to keep the players in line, and one of the masters at doing so was Hall of Fame coach Scott Bowman.

He would often lurk around the hotel lobby late at night to see if players were ignoring his standard midnight curfew. It was no accident that his teams often stayed in hotels that featured large granite or marble columns in their lobbies. Those columns gave Bowman something to hide behind.

The players, fully aware of Bowman's tactics, used to devise various means of countering them. They would come in through the parking garage or have a friend come downstairs to open one of the hotel's side exits that are usually locked at night. Or they would simply come in so late that Bowman had gone to bed.

Whatever tactic they used, the first step was always to do a furtive reconnaissance of the lobby from outside the hotel.

One of the things they looked for was the bottom of an overcoat sticking out from behind a pillar. Sometimes, Bowman would take a break from his surveillance, go for a walk, and come back to resume his post. But he didn't take off his overcoat.

If the players felt fairly sure that Bowman had taken the night off, they would just walk in and head for the elevator.

On one such night when Bowman was coaching the Montreal Canadiens, every player who entered was approached by the night porter, who had a hockey stick for them to autograph.

"Would you just sign it here please?" he asked the first player. When the next one came in, he said, "Could you just sign below where the other guy signed it?" The players, in typical NHL-player fashion, all complied.

The next morning, before practice, Bowman marched into the dressing room carrying a stick. "Here's who broke curfew by a little bit," he said, reading the first name. "Then the next guys to come in were . . ." and he moved down the stick, reading the names in chronological order. The night porter had also been good enough to mark down the times he had been required to leave his post to get an autograph.

According to the players on the team, the last name, entered around 4:30 a.m., was that of Peter Mahovlich. But Pete never confirmed that story.

•  •  •

Sometimes you hear people saying that something will never happen in hockey. It's best to remember that never is a long time.

It was fifty years ago – in 1962 – that Clarence Campbell, who was the president of the NHL at the time, was hearing the same kind of rumours that commissioner Gary Bettman hears today – speculation that the league was on the verge of expansion. At that time, Campbell's league operated only in Boston, Chicago, Detroit, Manhattan, Montreal, and Toronto. "There is a lot of casual talk about expansion," said Campbell, "but I'm not sure the NHL will ever include the west coast."

He was talking about Vancouver. The possibility of the NHL operating in places like Los Angeles, Anaheim, and San Jose was too ridiculous to even contemplate.

In the same interview, Campbell went on to say, "It must be understood that NHL hockey is luxury entertainment with tickets scaled from $2.50 to $5.00."

For the price of five cheap seats in those days, you can get a beer at a Toronto Maple Leafs home game today.

• • •

When Morden Lazarus wore his Stanley Cup ring, he always did so proudly.

It was a beauty, the one given to all the members of the 1977 Stanley Cup–winning Montreal Canadiens.

You've probably never heard of Morden Lazarus. If you know him at all, you probably know him better as Cookie. When your first name is Morden, a nickname is pretty well a necessity.

If you scan the roster of that 1977 championship team, you won't find a mention of either Cookie Lazarus or Morden Lazarus. But you will find Rick Chartraw. Cookie was his agent. Chartraw was a free spirit, to put it charitably, and in Montreal, where every hockey player is recognized as soon as he puts his nose out of the door, life was becoming somewhat stultifying. One of Chartraw's closest friends was Derek Sanderson, a fact that should tell you a lot about his lifestyle, and he was an American.

Put all these factors together and you come up with a guy who, by 1980, wanted to be traded.

The legendary Sam Pollock had departed by then, and in his place was Irving Grundman, a man whose primary involvement with sport before he got involved with the Canadiens was owning a bowling alley.

Chartraw told Grundman he wanted out. Nothing happened.

He pleaded with Grundman. Nothing happened.

He sent Cookie in to plead with Grundman. Nothing happened.

Chartraw was desperate. "If you can get me traded to Los Angeles," he said to Lazarus, "I'll give you one of my Stanley Cup rings."

Lazarus got Grundman's authority to broker a deal and somehow pulled it off. Chartraw became a member of the Los Angeles Kings and Cookie became the proud owner of a 1977 Stanley Cup ring.

●   ●   ●

Unfortunately, the story does not have a happy ending.

In April 1994, Peter Mahovlich was working for the Canadiens and living in Lazarus's house. He was part guest and part minder.

When a playoff round got unexpectedly extended, Mahovlich had to go on the road in a hurry. Lazarus was already out of town, and while the two of them were away, the house was burgled. Among the items stolen was the Stanley Cup ring. "The sentimental value of the ring was priceless," said Lazarus in February 2011, "and I'm still upset to this day that the break-in at my house took place that night that Peter had to leave, which resulted in the theft of the ring."

• • •

When Denis Savard was at his best, he was as shifty a forward as the game has ever seen. With the puck glued to his stick, he'd twist and turn, leaving defencemen in his wake.

One of the Hartford Whalers defencemen of the era – I'm pretty sure it was Adam Burt, but I may be wrong – was asked one of the standard questions by the media during training camp: "What's your goal for the upcoming season?"

"To stay out of the Denis Savard highlight film," he said.

• • •

Savard was always ready to look for an offensive opportunity, no matter what the situation might have been, and one night, coach Bob Pulford sent him out as the lone forward while his Chicago Blackhawks were facing a three-on-five situation.

The two defencemen were Norris Trophy–winner Doug Wilson and Bob Murray, now the general manager of the Anaheim Ducks.

In a situation like that, if the puck goes behind the opposition's net, you sit back and wait for the breakout to begin. Not Savard. He went after the puck and got it. Then he started one of his dazzling routines, darting back and forth, twisting and turning.

At one point, he looked up and nodded his head.

This was an established signal for a defenceman to go to the net for a pass. Wilson, who was also an offensive player of some repute, charged in from the blue line. But Savard had been on Murray's side of the ice when he nodded his head, so Murray dashed for the net as well.

At that point, Savard came out from behind the net and tried a wraparound.

The goalie went down and made the save. Wilson fell over the goalie. Savard banged into Murray, and they both went down.

Now, the three Blackhawks were lying on the ice watching the opponents enjoy a five-on-nobody break. Astonishingly, they didn't score.

"We all headed back to the bench with our sticks up," laughed Wilson afterwards. "We'd done our job. They didn't score."

But when they got to the bench, they discussed the play with Savard. "Why did you give us the nod if you were going to try a wraparound?" Wilson asked. "I didn't nod," said Savard. "My helmet had slipped down and I was just trying to get it back up."

• • •

Although Canadian fans were without the NHL for a year when Gary Bettman cancelled the 2004–05 season, they were at least left with some pleasant hockey memories.

In February 2002, Canada won the Olympic gold medal, the first such achievement in fifty years. In the springs of 2003 and 2004, Canada won the world championship. Then, in late summer of 2004, came the last gasp before the lockout, the World Cup tournament.

At this point, it was clear that the chances of the upcoming NHL season starting on time were remote – if indeed it started at all – so none of the major countries had any problems getting their players to participate.

The result was a superb tournament of high-class, high-speed, high-intensity hockey.

During the championship game between Finland and Canada, an inspired Team Finland scored a goal in the dying moments of the second period to take the game into the third with the teams tied 2–2.

A late goal like that is often devastating, but Canada responded with a goal from Shane Doan in the third period, then shut down the Finns the rest of the way to win the crown.

Afterwards, a sign was put up in the Canadian dressing room: "Practice is cancelled tomorrow. No one else left to beat."

# CHAPTER TWO

*Learning may be the best thing we have. It may be all that we can truly keep.*

Larry McMurtry, *Streets of Laredo*

**The first road trip** I made as a hockey writer started in Detroit – at the old Olympia Stadium. Having made a trip or two with the Montreal Expos, I assumed that hockey players travelled in the same manner as baseball players.

Accordingly, a few hours before the team's scheduled evening flight, I shuffled down to the deserted Montreal Forum, dropped my suitcase in the middle of the dressing room floor so it would be in plain view, and left.

Later, I went out to Dorval Airport and took the same commercial flight to Windsor as the Canadiens. The team bus was waiting at Windsor Airport to take us to the hotel in Detroit. I hadn't ridden on a hockey team bus before, so I just followed the other media guys aboard and took a seat in the part of the bus that was customarily for media use.

In baseball at that time, the coaches and manager sat at the front of the bus, with the media in the rows right behind. These days, the baseball media can sit where they want, as long as it's on their own bus. A separate vehicle is reserved for the team.

But on the Canadiens' bus in the Scott Bowman era, seating decorum followed a different format. The back row was for Bowman and his staff – in other words, for Bowman and assistant coach Claude Ruel. I subsequently learned that most hockey teams allocate the front seats to the coaching staff, just as baseball once did, but it was Bowman's theory that if he sat at the back, he could keep an eye on the players. If he sat at the front, there was no telling what they might be doing behind his back. The media sat in the two rows in front of Bowman, where he could also keep an eye on them.

When we got to the Hotel Pontchartrain in Detroit, I headed for the restaurant and, seeing that Dick Irvin was already there, went over to share a table with him while we awaited delivery of our luggage. That's the way it worked – and continues to work – in baseball: You leave your bags in the dressing room and the trainers load them with all the team's equipment, then deliver them to the hotel lobby in the next city. (At this point, methods diverge. Players pay a bellboy to take their luggage to their room. If they get caught carrying their own luggage by a teammate, there's a kangaroo-court fine. Newspaper guys, whose two favourite beers are Free and Free Lite, tend to carry their own bags.)

During our meal at the Pontchartrain, I asked Dick how much time the hockey trainers needed after our arrival to drop off our luggage. They would first need to go to the Olympia with the hockey equipment.

Dick was puzzled. "You're expecting the trainers to deliver your luggage?"

This was not a good sign. Even in 1973, Dick was already a veteran of hockey travel. And he wasn't known for his practical jokes. If he didn't understand what I was talking about, something was seriously wrong.

I explained what I had done. Dick found it somewhat amusing. "This is hockey, not baseball," he said. "In hockey, everybody carries his own bags."

As it happened, the Montreal trainers, Bob Williams and Eddy Palchak, had noticed the large Expos sticker on the suitcase that had mysteriously appeared in the middle of the dressing-room floor and figured out that it probably belonged to a misguided baseball writer. They had been kind enough to bring it along, but they made it clear that this was a unique occurrence and that, as Dick had pointed out, "This is hockey, not baseball. In hockey, everybody carries his own bags."

For me, this was a fundamental lesson. In hockey, you were never allowed to get too exalted an opinion of your worth. Everybody from Scott Bowman to Guy Lafleur to the latest call-up was responsible for his own luggage. You checked it in at the airport and you picked it up at the carousel. You carried it to the bus and you shoved it in the storage compartments under the bus. You took it from there to your hotel room. And so on.

Maybe I placed too much importance on the regimen, but it always seemed to me that this was not an unreasonable demand to make upon players. If you're going to be successful in hockey, you've got to accept your responsibilities. Whatever your job may be, whether it's to check or score or block the goalie's view, people are counting on you to do it. You can't expect someone else to do the drudgery any more than you can expect them to carry your luggage.

•   •   •

As general manager of the Colorado Avalanche, Pierre Lacroix was never the easiest hockey executive to deal with. All GMs have high opinions of themselves, but Lacroix seemed to go the extra mile in that regard. Furthermore, he held grudges. He stopped talking to me decades ago because I said on *Hockey Night in Canada* that his son Eric, who played for the Avalanche at the time, had been barred from a players-only meeting because of doubts as to whether he could be trusted.

It was true, of course, but Lacroix didn't think that the public had a right to know about it. He called my *Hockey Night* colleague John Davidson – not me – to complain. Afterwards, he settled into a long-term pout and wouldn't acknowledge my presence even if we were the only two people in an elevator – which we occasionally were.

This hardly mattered, though, as Lacroix never said anything to anglophones that was worth hearing.

He could also be difficult in his dealings with agents, and on one occasion, he frustrated Don Meehan, who was – and still is – the top agent in the game in terms of number of clients.

Meehan prides himself on being a deal-maker, always preferring conciliation to confrontation. Even when his clients, notably Scott Niedermayer and Mike Peca, engaged in serious battles with their teams – New Jersey and Buffalo respectively – and withheld their services for extended periods, they did so at their own insistence, not Meehan's.

In 1997, when Bob Clarke and Bob Gainey had been selected to put together the Team Canada that would compete in the Nagano Olympics, Lacroix let it be known that he was miffed because he hadn't been asked to take part.

At the time, Meehan was trying to negotiate a new contract for one of the Colorado players and was being frustrated at every turn. As a result, he wasn't feeling particularly charitable towards Lacroix.

"Bob Clarke and Bob Gainey are Hall of Famers," Meehan said one night when we were hoisting a pint or two in the Madison Pub. "Pierre Gauthier built the team that Lacroix inherited. What Lacroix has done could have been done by the Zamboni driver."

"That's a good line, Donny," I said. "Can I use it in the paper?"

"Sure," said Meehan. "Right now, I don't care if he gets mad at me. The negotiations aren't going anywhere anyway."

Needless to say, Lacroix saw Meehan's comment and was furious. The next time they met, there was what the diplomats call "a full and frank exchange of views." At high volume. But eventually the air was cleared and Meehan got his contract.

•   •   •

When Neil Smith took over as general manager of the New York Rangers in 1989, his goal, like that of every NHL GM, was to win the Stanley Cup.

The prospects weren't good. The Rangers hadn't won a Cup for decades. And if the exact date of that last Cup had slipped their memory, they were reminded every time they visited the Nassau County Coliseum and the New York Islanders fans serenaded them with singsong chants of "Nineteen Forty, Nineteen Forty."

Working in Smith's favour was the fact that the team's owners wanted a Cup as badly as he did and were willing to let him amass a number of high-priced stars. There was no salary cap in those days, but most teams tried to keep player costs as low as they could. That didn't seem to be a concern in New York.

As the St. Louis Blues owner, Harry Ornest, liked to say, "Neil Smith has an unlimited budget and he overspent it."

By 1991, the Rangers were showing signs of being serious Stanley Cup contenders, but they still needed that one key guy – someone who could get the various types of players to coalesce by giving the team the leadership it so badly needed.

Smith knew exactly who he wanted: Mark Messier, the captain of the Edmonton Oilers.

Messier had been in Edmonton through the glory years of the mid-eighties, and he was still there after owner Peter Pocklington eviscerated the team to fill his pockets in the late eighties. Messier was still in Edmonton in 1990 when he led an undermanned Oilers team to its fifth Stanley Cup in seven years. It was the dynasty's last gasp, and it was Messier who was the driving force behind the team's success.

Pocklington, recognizing Messier's worth, told Oilers general manager Glen Sather to move him out just like the others.

Smith rightly valued Stanley Cup experience and had already acquired Adam Graves from the Oilers. He went after Messier and, in what came as a surprise to the Oilers, was the only GM to express an interest even though everyone in the league knew that Messier was available.

Sather was not the easiest man to deal with. Even if he thought that he had arranged a good deal, he would try to get a little more, not because he was greedy, but just because it was his nature. He always liked to have the last laugh.

When the deal for Messier appeared to have been firmed up in the summer of 1991, Sather asked Neil Smith what further incentive the Rangers could offer. "If we win the Stanley Cup with Mark Messier," said Smith, "I'll kiss your ass in the front window of Macy's at high noon."

Sather laughed, said he would hold him to it, and agreed to the deal. Messier went to New York.

Today, Sather himself is GM of the Rangers, and he often passes Macy's and thinks of the arrangement. Smith never did fulfill his part of the bargain. He says that he just said it to give an indication of how much he coveted the idea of winning the Cup.

He's telling the truth, of course. But Sather still likes to relate the story – as always, just to get the last laugh.

•  •  •

The acquisition of Messier was the best move that Smith could have made. Messier was not only the best leader in hockey, he may have been the best leader in any sport. He had an imposing presence, he played hard, he came through when the team most needed a lift, and he would not accept anything less than a complete effort from his teammates.

He wasn't superb in every game. No one is. But he always made a contribution and he always gave everything he had.

It was in 1994 when the Rangers finally made their run at the Cup. Smith had put together the team he wanted, with Messier as its captain. He had the demanding Mike Keenan as coach and continued to work with him even though the two often didn't see eye to eye. They even sniped at each other publicly, a practice that delighted the voracious New York media.

The Rangers won the opening round of the playoffs. They won the second. Then came their biggest test – the conference final against their most intense rival, the New Jersey Devils.

At the time, the Devils' home was the Meadowlands, which, as the crow flies, is only about eight miles from Madison Square Garden. They were one of the league's powerhouses. In fact, they won the Stanley Cup the following season.

The series went back and forth, with the Devils winning three of the first five games. Prior to Game 6, with the Rangers facing elimination, Messier guaranteed a road win for his team. Not only was his prediction correct, he scored a hat trick to make sure it was correct.

The series moved back to Madison Square Garden for the deciding seventh game.

Despite his heroic performance in Game 6, Messier wasn't very good in Game 7. In fact, he was quite ineffective for most of the evening. But the Rangers got a goal, and in the dying minutes were desperately trying to hang on to a 1–0 lead.

With forty-eight seconds left to play, Messier lined up for the faceoff in his own end. This was something of a surprise.

Throughout the Edmonton Oilers' dynasty, Craig MacTavish took all those crucial defensive-zone draws. And MacTavish was playing for the Rangers at the time, as were three other Oilers with Cup rings: Esa Tikkanen, Glenn Anderson, and Kevin Lowe.

But Keenan, who hadn't been happy with the play of MacTavish and who loves to follow his hunches, sent out Messier to face the Devils' Bernie Nicholls. Messier was good on faceoffs but not great. On this occasion, Nicholls beat him cleanly.

The Devils, with goaltender Martin Brodeur on the bench, attacked furiously. Eventually, an icing call relieved the pressure.

Now there were twenty-four seconds left. Again Messier took the draw against Nicholls. Again Nicholls won. Again the Devils attacked, but Rangers goaltender Mike Richter caught the puck to stop play.

After a consultation, the clock was adjusted to show 18.6 seconds remaining in regulation time. In a show of confidence, Messier told his defencemen, Brian Leetch and Jeff Beukeboom, to switch sides. The implication was that he was not only going to win the faceoff, he was going to get the puck to Leetch.

Then he lost the draw again.

Beukeboom, playing out of position, tried to clear the puck but couldn't. The play remained in the Rangers' end and with 7.7 seconds left, Valeri Zelepukin poked home the tying goal.

The Rangers were devastated, totally demoralized. To come so close to victory and then see it slip away was a crushing blow.

After all, the series had opened in similar fashion with New Jersey scoring a last-minute, six-attacker tying goal. The Rangers were awful in the overtime of that game, and the Devils had won.

In a situation like this, coaches usually try to get to the team quickly before terminal morbidity starts to set in. The Rangers' coaches had followed that strategy in the first game. But this time, when they walked into the room, Messier was already talking.

It was not a pep rally. It was not a stirring oration. But he just kept talking, preventing his teammates from dwelling on the collapse.

Everything he said was positive. He told them they had played well and that they had contained the Devils' offence. He reminded them that for fifty-nine minutes of even-strength play, the Devils had been unable to score and that they wouldn't be able to pull their goalie in overtime.

He said that the Rangers would play all night if necessary, but they would do what needed to be done. He said they would go out and attack, that they had been poised and composed for the first sixty minutes.

He kept talking, like the hero in the old war movies, the guy who keeps the other survivors in the lifeboat awake until the rescuers arrive.

At one point, defenceman Kevin Lowe, who had been receiving medical treatment, entered the room. Looking as if the turn of events was exactly what he had hoped for, Lowe interrupted Messier to say that under these

circumstances, the win would be that much more enjoy-
able when it came.

Not if it came. When it came.

After about ten minutes, heads had lifted, slumped
shoulders had straightened. The gloom had dissipated.

These were not the beaten Rangers, cursed by fate to
snatch defeat from the jaws of victory. This was a team
that was going to create the most memorable game in
New York hockey history, the team that was going to
bounce back and produce a victory that was so stirring
that its legend would be passed down from grandfather to
father to son.

These were Mark Messier's Rangers. He was their
leader. He had guaranteed a win in Game 6 and had gone
out and delivered it.

Now Mark Messier was telling them that everything
was right with the world. They had done nothing wrong;
they had just added a touch of excitement, a touch of
glamour. They were the better team because Messier had
told them so, and who were they to argue?

Twenty-four minutes of playing time later, Messier
was proven right. He wasn't on the ice for the goal. He
had nothing to do with it. But he had everything to do
with it.

Seven games later, the Rangers won the Stanley Cup,
the only one they have won in seventy-one years.

•   •   •

In some sports, the team itinerary is sacrosanct. If the bus is to leave at noon, it leaves at noon. Not fifteen seconds past noon.

On one occasion back in the eighties, when I was occasionally covering some baseball, the team bus was pulling away from the hotel just as a player came running out of the front door. Seeing him, some of the players shouted to stop the bus. The manager, who is the person who makes decisions regarding the movements of any team bus, told the driver to keep going. I was told that such situations were not unusual. Each player – and media person – is given an itinerary at the start of the road trip, and as far as some managers are concerned, it is to be followed to the letter – or to the second, if you prefer.

I imagine that today's baseball managers are a little more flexible. Then again, considering what baseball players get paid these days, it's surprising that they need a bus at all. Just order up a string of limos, one per player.

Today's baseball players don't have to endure the suffering that afflicted their predecessors back in the eighties. In those days, the poor dears didn't always get to travel on charter flights, and sometimes had to rough it out in the first class section on commercial flights. If there weren't enough first class seats to accommodate the entire team, players had to sit in coach, but league rules stipulated that three seats had to be purchased for every two players.

It must also be mentioned that smoking was allowed on airplanes at that time. There was a separate section at the back for smokers, which always seemed remarkably silly to me – a bit like having a no-urinating section in a swimming pool.

As a result, it was not uncommon for some gasping, red-faced granny who had been stuck in the smoking section despite being a non-smoker to stagger up to the front and ask if she could have one of the vacant seats between ballplayers.

In every case I know of, they were quite adamant. That seat had been paid for and it belonged to them. It was to be kept vacant so that they could stretch out or play cards, or just use it as a storage area so they wouldn't have to suffer the inconvenience of reaching into the luggage rack when they wanted something out of their carry-on bag.

Hockey players did not travel that way. The twentieth century had almost ended before some NHL teams were spared the rigours of commercial travel and used charters exclusively. And when hockey players flew commercial, they were accorded one seat per player – in the back. Sometimes, the captain and a couple of veterans might get moved up to business class, but for the most part, hockey players sat in the back of the plane like everyone else. And they often got middle seats as well.

•   •   •

Travel with the Edmonton Oilers was probably the most easygoing in professional sports. As far as the Oilers were concerned, the itinerary was nothing more than a general advisory that could be adhered to as long as it didn't cause too much inconvenience.

If it said the bus was to leave at noon, it was generally considered wise to be somewhere near the hotel lobby by noon. That way, if a teammate reminded you that you'd forgotten something, you still had plenty of time to go back up to your room and get it.

It must be conceded that when he was coach, Glen Sather, like some baseball managers, would occasionally order the bus to pull away as a player came running out of the hotel. The difference, though, was that Sather, grinning ear to ear and very proud of his little prank, would order the bus to stop a block away.

Granted, it must also be conceded that when the player got within twenty yards of the bus, Sather might order the driver to pull away again, but sooner or later, the bus would stop long enough to let the panting player board. He had his sadistic moments, did Glen Sather. Not everyone understood the Oilers' ways.

In 1990, the team was playing a pre-season goodwill tournament in Düsseldorf, Germany. The itinerary said quite clearly that the team bus would leave for the rink at 2:00 p.m. At the appointed hour, not a single active player was on the bus. Bill Tuele, the team's public-relations manager, was not concerned. He was leaning back in his front row seat, waiting patiently.

Suddenly, there was the sound of air brakes being released and the driver putting the bus in gear. "You don't need to go yet," said Tuele. "We can wait a while."

The bus driver consulted his clipboard, looked at the sheet of paper, and looked at Tuele. He held the clipboard up for Tuele's perusal and pointed to the instruction sheet. "It says ve go at 2:00 p.m.," he pointed out.

"No, no," said Tuele. "It's okay. We'll wait."

"Ze order says two o'clock," said the bus driver. "It is two o'clock. Ve go."

And off he went. The Oilers' cavalier approach to timetables did not mesh well with legendary German efficiency.

•   •   •

In 2000, the National Hockey League adopted a two-referee system. There had been experiments with the concept the year before, but it made no sense to have one referee some nights and two on other nights.

Now, more than a decade later, most people accept the change. Ron MacLean doesn't, but Ron can be unreasonably stubborn on some points. The inescapable fact is that the game is far better with two referees than it was with one. For one thing, there's more room for the players. That may seem like a contradiction, but it isn't.

When there was one referee, he'd skate mostly between the blue lines. Once he got to a blue line, with the play flowing up alongside him, he'd curl back. But that's the area where a lot of plays germinate.

There are drop passes. There are attempts to maintain possession while other forwards head for the net. It's the area where the defending team tries to force the puck-carrier to make a decision and tries to put the play off-side. In the middle of all this, the referee was often banged around or, worse still, interfered with the play.

Under the two-referee system, one referee skates well ahead of the play and the other stays slightly behind. The back referee, therefore, doesn't get to the blue line at the same time as the puck.

Now it's up to the players to decide whether the attack continues or not. There is no referee in the middle of the play.

Granted, there are still occasions – much rarer than they used to be – when a referee gets caught in a scrum, but it's usually behind the net. His involvement there isn't likely to create an odd-man rush as it often did when the single referee inadvertently deflected a puck at the blue line.

In the single-referee era, you rarely saw a referee behind the net. He'd have too far to go if play went the other way in a hurry. Now, a referee is there most of the time, and as a result, he's in a position to determine if the puck crosses the goal line. Even though there are in-net cameras, overhead cameras, and isolated cameras, there are still occasions when it's not clear whether a puck crossed the goal line or stayed out.

On those occasions, the referee is almost always there to provide a definitive answer.

Could his determination be wrong? Yes, it could. But at least by encouraging a referee to be in such close proximity to the net, the league has put itself in a position to give the fans the best possible chance of the correct decision.

Another advantage of the system is increased discipline. With two sets of eyes watching the play, it's tougher to get away with a cheap shot. When there was one referee, he had to be up with the play keeping an eye on the puck. He couldn't watch what a couple of bad-tempered combatants were doing to each other two zones behind him.

With hockey being as fast as it is today and with so many big bodies moving around at high speeds, it's easy for one referee to have his view of an infraction blocked. With a second referee, the right call tends to be made. As a result, the game is more likely to stay under control. Nothing angers a hockey player more than being the victim of an unpunished serious infraction. His most likely response is to find a way to take justice into his own hands, and that's when all hell breaks loose.

Prior to 2000, there always seemed to be refereeing controversies in the playoffs and especially in the Stanley Cup final.

Now, those controversies are exceedingly rare. Certainly the replays have something to do with it. But so does the two-referee system. It stabilizes the game, whether Ron MacLean likes it or not.

•   •   •

The Montreal Canadiens, like many teams, often set up a luggage pool. While waiting for the luggage at the airport, everyone who wanted to be involved put in a dollar. (As far as I know, Ken Dryden never participated. It would take more than a luggage pool to get Kenny to part with a dollar.) The owner of the first suitcase to come onto the carousel or onto the luggage belt collected the pot.

The game was curtailed for a while after Yvan Cournoyer tried to claim the pot one day. The other players felt that even though Cournoyer's bag had been the first to appear, the fact that he was riding it when it came out of the baggage-handling area and onto the belt mitigated against his claim.

Cournoyer wasn't really trying to cheat. If he were, he wouldn't have come out riding his bag and grinning broadly. Still, the fact that the pool could be rigged created some trepidation.

Airport security in those days was not what it is today. If Cournoyer tried to go into a restricted area now, he'd probably end up in jail until he was too old to play any more.

# CHAPTER THREE

*People who have tried it tell me that a clear conscience makes you very happy and contented; but a full stomach does the business quite as well, and is cheaper, and is more easily obtained.*

Jerome K. Jerome, *Three Men in a Boat*

**In December 2010,** the Toronto Maple Leafs were having one of their usual bad nights. They had been hammered the night before in Pittsburgh and came home to produce their second poor showing within twenty-four hours.

The disgruntled Toronto fans were booing lustily midway through the second period, and as the game went on, they continued to express their displeasure. When the mismatch finally ended, with the Philadelphia Flyers cruising leisurely to a 4–1 victory, various items were thrown on the ice.

Littering the playing surface is not something that's often done by Leafs fans. There has been the occasional instance in the past – such as the time during the Harold

38

Ballard era when a disgruntled usher tossed his Maple Leafs cardigan on the ice – but usually nothing more than a few programs are jettisoned. Once in a long while, someone will throw a Leafs sweater over the glass.

Leafs fans are nothing like the students at Duke University in the United States, who try to make a point when they throw items onto the court at basketball games. I covered Duke in the NCAA final four once, and the students proudly told me of their activities. When playing one of those colleges noted for a high level of functional illiteracy among its players – and there are a good number of those in the United States – they threw pocket dictionaries. Facing a team that had an admitted druggie or two, they threw aspirins. When a team with some unmarried fathers visited Duke, they threw condoms. One night when I covered them, they were playing the University of Nevada Las Vegas and planned to throw all three.

Anything Toronto fans have done pales in comparison to the antics of the Duke students, but on the night of the Flyers' 4–1 victory, someone threw a square brown object onto the ice at the end of the game.

Later, on the local radio station, they played a clip of Toronto defenceman Francois Beauchemin saying, "I don't know what it was. It landed right on my stick."

One of the hosts on the radio show, former Columbus Blue Jackets general manager Doug MacLean, was lightning quick with his response. "Well, it wasn't a puck then," he said.

There was also an audio clip of Philadelphia defenceman Chris Pronger, who had been right beside Beauchemin
when the game ended. "It was a waffle," he said. "Honest. A
waffle. What kind of person takes a waffle to an NHL game?"

Good question, Chris. Here's a better one. What kind
of person spends more than $200 to watch the Leafs play?

• • •

Naturally enough, with Toronto fans being the idiots
savants of the hockey world, the throwing of a single pre-
packaged waffle received major play on the city's broadcast
media and in the sports sections of all the newspapers.

Billions of neurons were burned up by members of
the Leafs Nation attempting to determine the symbolism
lurking behind the hurling of one solitary waffle. There
were suggestions that it was hurled because it was soft and
therefore not unlike the Leafs. Or, perhaps because it was
square, the implication being that the Leafs would find it
easier to use than the round puck, which kept slipping off
their sticks. Or perhaps the Leafs were done like waffles, a
reference to the famous line delivered by Tiger Williams
back in the seventies when he said that the Leafs' playoff
opponents were "done like dinner."

In their next home game after the waffle incident,
thanks to a pair of early gift goals from Montreal back-up
goalie Alex Auld, the Leafs won (3–1 with an empty-
netter). The Eggo-Bomber did not strike.

But when they next played in the Air Canada Centre, they were easily handled by the Atlanta Thrashers. This time, with nine minutes left in the game and the Leafs trailing 5–1, a dozen waffles, the contents of a full box, we were later informed, landed on the ice.

The thrower was escorted out of the building and charged with mischief. Now the airwaves were full of pleas from hockey-show hosts urging fans not to toss garbage onto the ice.

One caller had the perfect answer. "Why not?" he asked. "Brian Burke does."

· · ·

The waffle-thrower, Joe Robb, was charged with mischief and, to the delight of the Toronto media, was expected to subsequently appear in court. It promised to be an entertaining story.

But a little more than a month after the incident, the Crown dropped the charges. In return for this largesse, Robb was ordered to do five hours of community service.

Furthermore, by decree of the company that owns the Leafs, Maple Leaf Sports & Entertainment, he was banned for life from all their sport facilities – the Air Canada Centre, BMO Field, and Ricoh Coliseum, which meant he couldn't watch live games of the Leafs, the Raptors, Toronto FC, or the Marlies.

Some of the hard-liners in the community were appalled. They felt he should have been punished for his actions, not rewarded.

•   •   •

There are worse things to throw on the ice than waffles. One of the Leafs' assistant general managers, Dave Poulin, who had a long and highly respectable career in the National Hockey League, recalled an incident when he was playing for the Philadelphia Flyers against the New York Rangers in Madison Square Garden.

He was lined up for a faceoff against Mark Pavelich when, out of the corner of his eye, he sensed some motion in an area where there should have been no motion – the space between himself and the infamous New York gallery gods. He stepped back from the circle just in time to avoid a large blue rat, which landed on the ice with predictable damage to the rodent. It was not a pretty sight.

This was not a plastic rat of the type thrown on the ice by Florida Panthers fans during the team's run to the Stanley Cup final in 1996. This was a real rat that had been covered with blue paint. "Immediately, questions about the guy who threw this came to mind," said Poulin. "One: We're midway through the third period. Did you bring this rat into the building and sit with it in your pocket for most of the game? Two: Did you catch this rat in Madison Square Garden? Three: If you caught the rat, did you just happen to have a can of Rangers-blue spray paint in your pocket?"

He never got an answer to any of the questions. But New York's airborne rat didn't come close to getting the amount of attention a few harmless waffles got in Toronto.

•  •  •

At least the rat was dead before it became the centre of attention (we think). During Game 3 of the 1975 Stanley Cup final between the Buffalo Sabres and Philadelphia Flyers – probably the weirdest playoff game in NHL history – a very much alive bat started flying around in the corner where a faceoff was to be held.

The players stood and watched the bat for a few seconds as it flitted about, looping and diving near the faceoff circle. But when it came close to Buffalo forward Jim Lorentz, he displayed the kind of hand-eye coordination that is an attribute of good forwards in the NHL. With one quick flick of his stick, he slugged the bat on the head and it fell to the ice dead.

No one rushed to pick it up. The players and the officials just stood and looked at it, not sure what to do. Finally, Flyers forward Rick MacLeish took the initiative. He picked it up bare-handed, skated over to the penalty box, and dropped it over the boards.

•  •  •

But there was more to come that night. It was baking hot in Buffalo, and with a full house in the old Memorial Auditorium, the temperature rose steadily. As a result, clouds of fog blanketed the ice. When conditions got so bad that the puck couldn't be seen, someone brought bed sheets out from under the stands – why there would be bed sheets there is a good question – and the players skated around holding sheets extended between them in order to get the fog to dissipate.

Lorentz said afterwards that he whacked the bat because he was afraid it would get into the hair of team-mate Don Luce, who sported a massive Afro.

Whatever the reason, he was forever after known in hockey circles as Batman.

• • •

Olympia Stadium was a throwback to the days of the six-team league, an era when the players were so poorly paid that the owners didn't need luxury boxes to make a hefty profit.

It was a cozy building with good sight lines, and the press box was Spartan, basically a two-tiered affair stuck in the stands.

The writers who covered the Red Wings' home games on a regular basis were given the seats in the front row. The visiting writers and anybody else who didn't really matter much got the back row. As far as facilities were concerned, there was no real difference. You could still see the game from the second row and the work spaces were the same size on both rows.

The problem was that Jack Dulmage of the *Windsor Star* had a seat in the front row, and he never missed a home game. Dulmage was a good hockey writer. In fact, he was on the executive of the Professional Hockey Writers Association. Unfortunately, he was also a pipe smoker. Every fifteen minutes or so, Dulmage would go through that ritual that pipe smokers love – the meticulous tapping, scraping, stuffing, and tamping. Then came the climax. He would light his pipe, sending out more smoke than the British Navy created at the Battle of Jutland. Or – for those of you who are less historically inclined – more smoke than an Icelandic volcano.

Those of us sitting behind Dulmage would try not to lose track of the game while we gasped, coughed, and wiped our watering eyes.

Dulmage would puff contentedly for five minutes or so, blissfully sending more plumes of noxious smoke towards the second row before putting down the pipe. Like all unattended pipes, it would then expire.

But, ten minutes later, he'd pick up the pipe and go through the whole routine again.

I think I may have seen some memorable moments in the old Detroit Olympia. But I don't remember any. All I remember is Jack Dulmage's pipe.

•   •   •

When it comes to developing its fan base, the National Hockey League is missing a good bet. Literally.

"I am opposed to gambling in all its forms," NHL commissioner Gary Bettman has said. This is clearly not a stance that has been handed down from his forbears. His brother, Jeffrey Pollack, is commissioner of the World Series of Poker.

Bettman strongly opposed the sports lotteries when they were introduced in Canada, and at his insistence, the NHL even initiated court proceedings against the province of Ontario to try to prevent Sport Select from offering NHL games on its menu.

I once asked him why he took this stance. I pointed out that many hockey fans love to gamble. Hockey pools are as much a national sport in Canada as hockey itself. I tried to convince him that by encouraging fans to get involved in pools and gambling sites, he could increase his television ratings. Fans with a bet on a game would be much more likely to tune in than fans with no financial interest in the outcome. Similarly, fans who have picked certain players in a pool are much more likely to follow that player's production than fans who are not in a pool. Bettman would have none of it. "Those aren't the kind of fans we want to develop," he said.

Who knew that the NHL could be so choosy? When Nielsen ratings are released, they don't say, "Two million viewers watched, but half a million of those were only watching to see how their bet did." Apparently those minuscule ratings that the NHL has pulled in on the third-rate networks Bettman managed to find as homes for the NHL are ideal because they're the "right kind" of viewers.

Has Bettman ever considered why the National Football League is so popular? It certainly isn't because the games are invariably thrilling. In fact, many of them are a crashing bore. The outcome of many is determined before halftime. But if the spread is fifteen and a team is up by seventeen, millions of fans with a bet on the game will stay glued to their sets for the second half, even though the outcome is hardly in doubt.

The NFL is a betting league. The games usually run for about three hours and fifteen minutes. But only sixty minutes of that time is the game itself. And of those sixty minutes, a large portion is spent watching the team huddle or waiting for the ball to be snapped. You can catch up on a lot of reading during an NFL game and not miss a moment of action.

Yet NFL ratings are astronomical, so much so that what was once a Sunday afternoon league has now spread to Sunday night as well as Mondays and Thursdays. And once the college season ends, Saturday games appear on the schedule as well.

The people who run the NFL never come right out and admit that theirs is a betting league. But it's not hard to tell what they think. Injury reports have to be filed on a regular basis. If any team is judged to be messing with its evaluations – listing a player as "questionable" when he should in fact be listed as "probable" for instance – a heavy fine is levied.

The NFL is aware that big gamblers want to know who is likely to play and who isn't, so it makes sure that every effort is made to keep those gamblers happy.

What happens in the NHL when a player is injured? We get a laughable "lower-body injury" report with no estimate of the amount of time the player is likely to miss.

This is the twenty-first century. I mention this just in case Gary Bettman ends up reading this. He apparently hasn't noticed yet.

Gambling is everywhere. Casinos are springing up all over North America. Poker shows, likes the ones his brother's enterprise turns out, are staples on the sports networks. Off-shore betting sites are available to anyone with a credit card and internet access.

Even Bettman's own product – whether he likes it or not – has a heavy gambling involvement. *Hockey Night in Canada* runs its own pool, for instance, and gives out the weekly results during its Saturday night telecast. Almost every rink in the NHL has board advertising for a casino, a sports lottery, or a gambling site.

Marian Ilitch owns a casino in Detroit. Her husband owns the Detroit Red Wings. But Bettman is quick to point out that Marian is not involved in the Red Wings. Of course not, Gary. Marian would never have anything to do with the Wings. Granted, she used to sign all the multi-million-dollar paycheques for the Wings, but now she's gone cold turkey and never says a word to her hubby about his hockey team. And he never mentions her casino.

Instead of working so hard to tilt at gambling's windmills, the NHL should be embracing the concept of sports betting. For example, why not offer $10,000 a week as a hockey pool prize? You pick ten players, say, and if your ten players get more points from Sunday morning to Saturday night than anyone else, the NHL gives you $10,000.

There would be no real hint of impropriety. The league is giving away $10,000 either way. It's not likely that anyone would have reason to accuse the league of somehow rigging the results. It you wanted to engage in that sort of activity and risk the consequences, surely you'd need more than $10,000 as motivation.

Heck, they could make it $100,000 a week and really get some attention. That would cost the league about $4 million a year, but so what? That's $133,000 per year per team. It wouldn't even be noticed on the balance sheet, but it would certainly get noticed by thousands, perhaps millions, of borderline hockey fans who would then start to tune in to games to see how their picks are doing.

Why not start to give gamblers some degree of disclosure regarding injuries, as the NFL does? The excuse that is most common in the NHL – that a player would subsequently be targeted – is nothing short of idiotic. Does an NFL player coming back from a knee injury get his knee targeted? Can't you just hear the NHL announcers now? "Oh, look, they're hacking away at Ovechkin's groin

with their sticks because they know he just came back
from a groin injury."

The NHL churns out lots of statistical information and
puts it on its website. Why not have someone examine those
stats and put together those esoteric bits of trend information that the gamblers like? They could point out that a
given team hasn't beaten its upcoming opponent in the last
ten Friday games in odd-numbered months, and so on.

What Bettman seems to be unable to realize is that his
league is in no position to be picky about the kind of
viewers it attracts. Despite his failed attempt on a number
of occasions to keep the players' salaries down, they keep
going up. If the owners are to be able to pay those salaries
and if the league is to avoid more labour strife when the
current collective bargaining agreement expires, the league
badly needs TV numbers. The game the players produce is
excellent, but more fans need to be drawn in to watch the
games and find this out for themselves.

If the NHL were to court the gamblers instead of shun-
ning them, it would have a lot better chance of attracting
more fans. The commissioner's views on gambling should
have nothing to do with it.

•   •   •

This story did not come from Wayne Gretzky. Over the
years, Gretzky has let me in on a lot of behind-the-scenes
stories, but if the anecdote had the potential to embarrass

someone, he always made sure that it was off the record. This one, however, comes from a teammate of Gretzky from the 1993 Los Angeles Kings.

The setting is the warm-up prior to Game 7 of the Campbell Conference championship between the Kings and the Toronto Maple Leafs. A teammate, sensing that Gretzky was not his usual self, skated over to him and asked what was wrong. "Nothing," growled Gretzky.

The teammate skated away, thinking that perhaps Gretzky was just feeling the tension. The winner would be going to the Stanley Cup final against the Montreal Canadiens. The loser would be going golfing.

He continued to watch Gretzky and became more certain than ever that something was amiss. Again he queried Gretzky, and again Gretzky insisted he was fine. "Look, I know you," said the teammate. "I know something's got you upset. What is it?" Gretzky finally opened up. He said he hadn't had his usual game-day afternoon nap because he had twice been awakened by the telephone.

In each case, the caller was his wife, Janet. She normally wouldn't phone at that time of day but had done so because she was being relentlessly pestered by Mike Myers, who wanted a ticket to the game. Tickets were so much in demand that being a Hollywood star wasn't good enough. You had to be a Wayne Gretzky. So Gretzky got Myers a ticket.

"So that's it?" said the teammate. "You missed your nap?"

"No, that's not it," said Gretzky. "Look at him."

He pointed to the seat where Myers was sitting – wearing a No. 93 Doug Gilmour Toronto Maple Leafs sweater.

"Gretz was so mad at that," said the teammate, "he got all fired up. He was up for that game to begin with, but this pushed him to the limit."

Gretzky got a hat trick that night, and the Leafs were eliminated. Toronto fans still blame referee Kerry Fraser, saying that Gretzky should have been kicked out of the game when his stick accidentally clipped Gilmour. "If the fans really knew what went on," laughed Gretzky's teammate, "they wouldn't have blamed Kerry Fraser all these years. They'd have blamed Mike Myers."

•  •  •

It's not often that the head of a powerful association can say he sent one of his predecessors to jail. But when Paul Kelly took over as executive director of the National Hockey League Players' Association (NHLPA) in 2007, he was fully qualified to make that statement.

Kelly had everything the NHL players were seeking. He was familiar with the sport, even though he had never held a hockey-related job.

I knew him well. I covered the trial in 2000, when Marty McSorley was charged with assault in a Vancouver court after using his stick to whack Donald Brashear on the head. Kelly was McSorley's lawyer, and we'd occasionally have lunch together during the trial.

Previously, when Kelly was a prosecutor in Massachusetts, we had also compared notes on many of Alan Eagleson's transgressions. He persevered against strong opposition in building a case against Eagleson, the founding executive director of the NHLPA, finally striking a plea bargain that saw Eagleson plead guilty to three counts of mail fraud in 1998. Eagleson was fined $700,000 and pleaded guilty to three more counts of fraud in a Toronto court. He admitted that he had embezzled proceeds from the Canada Cup tournaments of 1984, 1987, and 1991. He was sentenced to eighteen months in a minimum-security prison but served no more than six months. Eagleson was supported right to the end by powerful Canadian political figures and was all but bulletproof north of the border.

Even after his conviction, he went off to jail smiling broadly and waving to his supporters in the courtroom. Veteran Canadian court watchers said they had never before seen anyone in that situation who did not leave the courtroom in handcuffs.

Those in the know said that this should have been Canada's Watergate, that the corruption spread far beyond a hockey executive and involved Supreme Court judges, cabinet members, the RCMP, and even a former prime minister or two. But it ended with Eagleson waving to his powerful friends as he went to "jail."

Kelly was immune to Canadian pressure, and along with such people as Russ Conway of the *Lawrence*

*Eagle-Tribune* and former NHL player Carl Brewer, pursued Eagleson relentlessly.

When Eagleson was finally sentenced in a Boston court, Brewer stood up and said, "Thank God for the United States of America, because this could never have happened in Canada."

It could never have happened without Paul Kelly either.

●   ●   ●

Kelly became the fourth head of the NHLPA, and two of the previous three, Eagleson and Ted Saskin, were bounced for acts that were considered to be against the best interests of the union.

As a result, the NHL players badly wanted to get someone whose reputation was above reproach, and in Kelly, that is exactly what they got. There was also a feeling that the PA needed a strong leader to mend the rifts created by the 2004–05 lockout.

Saskin assumed control during that lockout when players mutinied against then executive director Bob Goodenow – though their salaries had increased tenfold during his regime.

But two years into the new collective bargaining agreement, players realized that Saskin had agreed to what could have been a terrible deal had the owners not followed their usual course of self-destruction.

In Paul Kelly, they picked a guy who knew how to strike

the proper balance. He knew the difference between right and wrong. He knew how to get the best possible deal for those who employed him, and he promised to do just that. He also promised to be a caretaker for the game. Owners tend to care about nothing but profit. Players like their money, too, but if anybody was going to stand up for the game, it was going to be the union. It all seemed so rosy.

Less than two years later, Kelly was fired. There was no good reason. It was just due to a power struggle within the PA. With Kelly gone, the organization went into a death spiral as the survivors, no longer having Kelly to attack, attacked each other. It took almost two years for the PA to get sufficiently reorganized to have any meaning whatsoever, and to install Don Fehr, the former head of the baseball players' union, as a successor to Kelly.

Kelly is now the executive director of College Hockey Inc., an American organization that promotes college hockey as an alternative to the junior ranks.

# CHAPTER FOUR

*Nothing is more predictable than the media's parroting of
its own fictions and the terror of each competitor that it
will be scooped by the others, whether or not the story is
true because quite frankly, dears, in the news game these
days, we don't have the staff, time, interest, energy, liter-
acy or minimal sense of responsibility to check our facts by
any means except calling up whatever has been written by
other hacks on the same subject and repeating it as gospel.*
John le Carré, *The Tailor of Panama*

**When you're in the media business,** you become
accustomed to young people coming up to you and saying
that they would love to have a job like yours and that they
feel they are qualified to do it. What they're really saying
is that they think they could do your job better than you
do, but that's all right.

There's nothing wrong with ambition.

The problem is that they don't really understand what
the job requires. They think that because they can spout
off a number of statistics, can recite all the Stanley Cup

winners since 1950 in order, and know all the clauses in
the NHL rule book, they are qualified to be a hockey
columnist or a TV analyst.

What they don't realize is that every single one of
those attributes that they consider to be important is
available to everyone in the media. The statistics are contained in the NHL's *Official Guide*, which is distributed to
every qualified member of the media at the beginning of
each season. The rules are in the rule book, also distributed annually to the media.

The NHL does not, however, distribute a number of
other job skills, each of which is necessary for anyone
hoping to be successful in the business. Here are some of
the vocations for which you have to be at least partly qualified if you want to make it in the hockey media:

*Doctor:* Do you know the difference between the
medial collateral ligament, the lateral collateral ligament,
and the anterior cruciate ligament? You'll need to. Do you
know how long it normally takes to recover from operations on each of them? You'll need to know that too. Do
you know all the long-term effects of concussion? If you
do, congratulations. You can make lots of money, because
no one else does.

Studies concerning the effect of concussions are
ongoing, and even though there are still a lot of aspects
that are not yet understood, our knowledge is evolving
every day. If you're in the media, especially the hockey and

football media, you have to keep abreast of all developments because what you presented five years ago as the
accepted belief – or even what you presented one year
ago – is not necessarily the case today.

And there are all the other common medical problems
that arise these days. What is a high-ankle sprain, and as
far as recuperation is concerned, how does it compare to a
broken ankle? How long is a player likely to be out with
a separated shoulder? Does such an injury always require
an operation? The list goes on.

*Travel agent*: If you're going to follow a team around,
especially during the most important time of the season,
the playoffs, you have to be able to change your travel
plans in a hurry.

You could, for instance, cover the first two games of a
series and have made plans to leave the following morning
only to discover that the superstar who was hurt the night
before is in hospital in serious condition and the team is
holding a press conference at the time your flight is scheduled to leave. If you think this sort of thing doesn't happen,
think back to the time Peter Forsberg had to have his
spleen removed. That was just one of the more high-
profile instances, but unexpected developments often
force a revision of travel schedules.

If you're going to do your job properly, your plans have
to be flexible, and as often as not, if you leave matters to
the company travel agent, you'll be heading to the next city

on a four-leg routing via Mongolia because it's cheaper. (If you fly with Air Canada, your luggage will probably take that routing anyway, but that's another story.)

You don't want to miss the press conference, but on the other hand, you can't allow yourself to get to the next city too late to catch up to what transpired there during the day.

There's also the crucial matter of frequent flyer points. One of the unofficial nicknames of the Professional Hockey Writers Association is "Points 'R' Us," and you certainly don't want to be travelling on Delta if your allegiance is to American Advantage, even if there is no appreciable difference between the itineraries the two airlines offer.

*Lawyer:* Unfortunately, you need to know something about the law. Fortunately, this won't make you a lawyer, so you can still have friends.

But really, to be in the sports media these days, you need to know a lot about the law.

It's not just a matter of figuring out how long a term Gary Bettman's latest recruit as an owner is likely to serve for fraud. You have to know the implications of everything from common assault to the attempted hiring of a contract killer. And you have to know how the laws in Canada differ from the laws in the United States. And sometimes you need to know about European laws.

You also have to have an insight into labour law. Every time the collective bargaining agreement with the players comes up for renewal, the various facets of labour law as they relate to professional sports emerge as a subject for discussion because they will have an impact upon negotiations.

You have to know a lot of the general tenets of the law, even if not the specifics. You should know, for instance, that a contract is never the last word. As far as some people are concerned, a contract is just one step in the negotiation process. The next step is a courtroom battle or a renegotiation. Furthermore, the fact that someone made a concession in a contract doesn't necessarily matter. You can't sign away your rights, and if that's what you did by making the concession, you're off the hook.

If you're going to be in the sports media, dealings with lawyers are unavoidable. Being what they are, lawyers will try to put their own slant on any matter. It is always helpful to be able to screen out the obfuscation or, as some might put it, ignore the lies when you're presenting the story.

One of the lawyers' favourite dodges, for instance, is to say that they can't discuss an issue "because it's before the courts." The truth, however, is that there is no ban on discussing an issue that's before the courts as long as the discussion doesn't prejudice the case. If you're a lawyer and can't figure out what's prejudicial and what isn't, maybe you're in the wrong profession.

*Computer technician:* It always seems that your laptop works perfectly when you're at home and then goes wonky when you're on the road. I've often thought that because laptop manufacturers enjoy such a lucrative market in the media, they should make a computer that stands up to having beer spilled on it.

But laptops get banged around during travel. They get dropped by the troglodytes in airport security. They get bounced around in the overhead racks where flight attendants insist they must be stowed for take-off and landing.

They're exposed to temperature extremes. They get left in locked cars during the hot months in the southern states. They get carried from the parking lot to the arena in Edmonton in the winter. And if you don't think that's a temperature extreme, you've never been in Edmonton in the winter.

One night in Edmonton, I started out on a four-block trek with Lance Hornby of the *Toronto Sun*. It seemed like a good idea at the time because (a) we were going to a bar and (b) the owner of the bar was the Oilers' Kevin Lowe, who had promised us free beers.

We managed to go two blocks before we gave up. Well, we didn't actually give up. The accumulated lure of (a) plus (b) was a bit too strong. But we did have to go into a Tim Hortons and stand around stomping our feet for ten minutes trying to warm up. Then we made the last two-block dash and barely got to the bar without freezing to death.

But I digress. Back to the laptops. There are various things that can be done to fix them after the mandatory first step – cursing loudly at them – has failed to do the job. I won't go into the details here, but let's just say that it helps to have a bit of computer expertise if you want to survive on the hockey beat.

*Player agent:* Even though there's a bit of overlap with the lawyer category in this one, not all agents are lawyers. Some, such as Gilles Lupien, who represents Martin Brodeur and Roberto Luongo, are former players. Pat Brisson, who numbers people like Sidney Crosby, Daniel Alfredsson, Patrick Kane, and the Sedin twins among his clients, used to wash cars for a living.

Some agents started out as financial advisors. Some are player relatives. For much of his career, Eric Lindros was represented by his father, Carl, who made it clear that he had no intention of taking on any other clients.

Anyone working in the media business can tell you that if you're going to deal with players, you're going to have to deal with agents. And if you're going to deal with agents, you have to be able to discuss player-related issues on their terms and in their language. You have to know the main clauses in the collective bargaining agreement, you have to understand the relationship between the player and the NHL Players' Association, and you have to be aware of the options that are open to a player in any dispute he might have with his team.

The only way to accomplish all those things is to be something of an agent yourself.

*High-level entrepreneur:* If you're in the media, you're never going to become a multi-millionaire. Even amassing a single million is highly unlikely, although I know some people who have done it. They didn't do it from the money they earned as hockey writers, though. They did it from sidelines such as writing drama, in the case of Rejean Tremblay, or through real-estate investments, in the case of a number of Vancouver writers who bought houses twenty-five years ago. There was even a New York–area hockey writer who won a lottery.

But not having big money doesn't stop you from understanding the thought processes of people who do have big money. We're talking about the owners of NHL teams here, and the largest single difference between them and the rest of the hockey world is that, for the most part, they are not hockey fans. They don't care whether their team wins or loses. They just want a profit. The healthier the better.

Canadian fans say, for instance, that the NHL should have teams in Quebec and southern Ontario. Naturally enough, they are thinking like fans. Owners, who think like owners, say, "Not a chance."

I'll explain those thought processes a little further on in the book, but the point here is that if you want to broaden the knowledge of your readers or viewers, you have to be able to explain why the owners feel the way they do.

You can't do that by quoting statistics or rhyming off the Stanley Cup winners for the last fifty years in order.

•  •  •

People have often asked whether the "Hotstove" segment of *Hockey Night in Canada* was scripted. Not only was it not scripted, but it rarely followed the rough outline that we mutually agreed upon before the show started.

In the earlier years, when I did the segment with John Davidson and Jim Hughson, we normally taped the show at 3:00 p.m. JD was the colour man on the New York Rangers telecasts and was therefore unavailable for a live show on Saturday night. But he was such an ideal panellist that no one ever gave the slightest thought to replacing him.

However, after JD had moved on to become the president of the St. Louis Blues and I was in the midst of one of my sabbaticals – in other words, I'd been fired again – the decision was made to air the show live.

It made good sense. The internet had blossomed, and newspaper guys could no longer dig up a story and sit on it until the paper's next edition.

News broke at any hour of any day, and the danger of having "Hotstove" ignore a major story that had broken during the five-hour window between the taping and the second intermission was too real to be ignored.

Worse still, what if the "Hotstove" panellists, in their 3:00 p.m. taping, discussed what had been a contentious issue – such as a decision on a suspension – only to have the league resolve the issue at 6:00 p.m.?

By the time I was doing the show with Pierre LeBrun

and Mike Milbury, it was always live, which had its good and bad points. While there was no risk of having the show look dated, there was a serious risk of having it lose its sparkle. Although we didn't re-tape often in the early days, when we did, the second version was invariably better than the first.

Sometimes you can get carried away making your point. Or you can drone on about something that may be interesting to you, but not to the viewer. Or you can slip up and use an expletive that the CBC doesn't like to have broadcast. That happened once during a first taping. And it wasn't JD or Jim who did it.

But with live TV, what you see is what you get, and on more than one occasion, we would get up from the desk after the lights were dimmed and agree that the show could have been a lot better, but we had let it get away from us.

For the viewers on those nights, a canned version would definitely have been preferable. But on other nights, the increased tension that comes from knowing that whatever you do is going out coast to coast, whether it is good or not, makes the show better.

•  •  •

The constant in both versions of the "Hotstove" was Ron McLean. And therefore, that meant that the other constant was that we had only the loosest of ideas about the direction the show would take.

Before every show, we'd meet Ron and tell him what we wanted to discuss. Usually, two of us dug up items. In the first incarnation, JD and I did it. In the later show, it was Pierre and me. The other guy just said, "I'll talk about whatever you guys want to talk about." That was no big problem. In both cases, they were able to add something to the matter at hand.

Ron would then ask us which of the stories we liked best, and we'd arrive at a rough prioritized list.

Then Ron would say something along the lines of "Okay, Pierre, we'll start with you on the Canadiens trade, then Mike can chime in on the headshot controversy, and then Al on the battles in the Chicago front office. Then we'll go on to the other items."

Agreement all around.

We'd get miked up, take our seats, and get a final makeup touch-up. The show would start, and Ron would welcome the viewers, look at the panellists, and say, "Well, Al, what's all this about dissension on the Los Angeles Kings?"

Let me tell you, it's not easy to rattle off something coherent about dissension on the Los Angeles Kings, which, if it was on the list at all, was one of the last items, and smile benignly at the camera while holding back visions of planting an axe in Ron's forehead.

•  •  •

I don't mean to imply that Ron did that sort of thing only to me. He does it to everybody. Everybody on the "Hotstove" that is. He doesn't do it to Don Cherry because Don will tell him on the air that he has screwed up.

At least, I'm pretty sure that's the case, because I know Don. But in recent years, I wasn't allowed to be around when Ron and Don were making up their list. By order of the executive producer at the time, Sherali Najak, I was to stay away from Don until after he had done his segment.

This was no arbitrary ruling, and here's how it came about: Ron habitually comes into the studio in mid-afternoon and gets miked up. It's a remote mike with a little antenna that's attached to the back of his collar, so it has no wires attached. Ron is free to walk wherever he wants.

As a result, from that moment on, the producer in the control room can eavesdrop on any conversation Ron might have simply by turning on the access to his mike. Don arrives in the building a bit later, but he rarely strays far from Ron.

Sometimes, since Don and I have been friends for more than thirty-five years and even went on vacation together once in England, I'd wander in to chat with him and Ron. Because Don and I share the same political views, our chats would sometimes turn into a discussion of the latest outrage being perpetrated upon the populace by left-wing politicians, liberal judges, or lunatic-fringe protesters.

Don is never one to hide his emotions, and sometimes he'd get so worked up that he was still thinking about the matters we had discussed when "Coach's Corner" started.

By virtue of being able to hear our conversations through Ron's mike, Sherali determined that I was the root of the problem and that the best way to make sure Don remained focused was to keep me away from him until his segment was finished.

Hence the ban.

• • •

While we're on the subject, it's time to correct at least one of the many injustices that are regularly hurled in Don's direction.

Whenever he does something controversial, his critics, usually those with left-leaning tendencies, demand that he be silenced. Their most common complaint is that it's outrageous that this man, "who is being paid with our tax dollars," should be allowed to air views that disagree with theirs.

The fact of the matter is this: "Coach's Corner" on *Hockey Night in Canada* is the single most-watched segment on Canadian television.

Most televised segments of this type have an opening intro, followed immediately by the show itself. "Coach's Corner" has such an intro, but it's followed by a commercial. A lucrative commercial.

Don Cherry's salary doesn't come from the taxpayers. It comes from the people who pay big bucks to sponsor his segment. And after he has been paid, there's lots left over to go into the CBC coffers.

Don Cherry doesn't cost the taxpayers any money. Don Cherry saves the taxpayers money.

# CHAPTER FIVE

*It is a capital mistake to theorize before one has data.*
Sir Arthur Conan Doyle, "Scandal in Bohemia"

**Hockey players always seem** to go through life with a light-hearted approach to even the most serious matters.

Tomas Vokoun had been having trouble moving at the level required of an NHL goaltender and finally had the problem diagnosed as pelvic thrombophlebitis, a potentially fatal condition.

It put him out of action for six months, a layoff that would elicit much moaning and whining from many an athlete, but Vokoun approached it with typical hockey-player aplomb. "It's a lot better to find out the way we did than in an autopsy report," he said.

• • •

I was sitting in a pub a full decade after Wayne Gretzky retired when a hockey fan came over and started chatting.

That was fine. It happens all the time, and on most

70

occasions, I enjoy talking to fans. Most of them are pleasant, and after we've exchanged a few words, they go on their way.

This one wasn't unpleasant, but he did insist on increasing my understanding of hockey. My feeling in this regard is that if I'm going to descend on someone I don't know because he has an area of expertise, I'm going to seek advice, not give it.

But he knew that I was a great admirer of Wayne Gretzky and wanted to let me in on a secret that had previously been withheld from me. When Gretzky played, he insisted, there was a league rule that said he couldn't be hit.

I mention this not because this view is unusual. Quite the contrary. Unfortunately, it's widespread. And it's not just regarded as a rumour. A lot of people genuinely believe it.

"So how would this work?" I asked. Would the referees be instructed by the NHL head office to warn teams that it was against the rules to hit Gretzky? Would the league distribute one of those memos that it sends out occasionally, the kind that has to be posted on team bulletin boards? And if that were the case, why has no player ever come forward to reveal this secret, even ten years after Gretzky left the game?

What would happen if someone ignored the rule? If Gretzky were to get hit, would a penalty then be issued?

Apparently, this is what my new-found friend believed. The rule was there, he said, but since nobody ever hit Gretzky, there was no need to call the penalty.

I then asked him if this was just a regular-season rule or if it applied in the playoffs as well. When the playoffs rolled around, what did coaches say to their teams? It must have been something along the lines of "This is it, guys. We're all starting fresh. We have just as much chance as anybody to win the Stanley Cup. Go out and give it everything you've got. Just one thing though. If you have to hit Gretzky to do it, forget about it. It's better to lose. Let someone else win the Stanley Cup."

And what about the players? They too must have talked about the limitation that had been imposed on them. The team leaders would have tried to urge their teammates on to greater effort in order to avoid elimination, "but not if you have to hit Gretzky."

The concept is so stupid, it defies belief. And yet, I hear it a lot.

The reason that Gretzky didn't get hit did not involve any convoluted plot or any secret league edicts.

For one thing, he played a lot of lacrosse when he was growing up and learned how to roll off checks. Other notable players who exhibited the same trait were Gary Roberts, Joe Nieuwendyk, and Brendan Shanahan.

The most important factor, though, was that Gretzky always had someone on his team who would take a very dim view of any overly exuberant check on Gretzky.

A quote from Ken Baumgartner, an enforcer of some repute, comes to mind. It was during the 2004–05 lockout, and there had been some suggestion that some players might cross the picket line. "They might," conceded Baumgartner, "but we'll be back some day, and you have to remember that hockey is a game that lends itself very well to retribution."

In the early days, Gretzky had Dave Semenko on his team. Then came Marty McSorley. Neither dealt in half measures. As far as they were concerned, there was a very low tolerance for physical assaults on Gretzky. "And what was really important," McSorley said, "was that you had to let them know that you didn't mind taking a suspension. If you hit Gretz, the retaliation might be more than just a fight. There could be something more tacked on. Someone could get hurt. If I got suspended, I didn't mind. I let them know that."

By the time Gretzky and McSorley parted ways, Gretzky was one of the elder statesmen of the league.

Players of that ilk don't have to put up with serious checking. That was true not only for Gretzky but also for people like Joe Sakic, Peter Stastny, Igor Larionov, and dozens of others.

There was never a Protect Gretzky Rule. But lots of people still think there was.

•   •   •

These days, most communication between hockey writers and the general managers is done through texting. In many ways, this is a distinct improvement over the earlier era when we had to phone them because in those days, GMs were often away from their offices, and getting a response could take a lot of time.

The GMs might be travelling with their team, they might be off in some remote part of the planet doing some scouting, or they might simply be in another part of the arena. And in some cases, it was a good bet that they would be on a golf course.

Before cell phones, the customary approach was to call a GM in his office, fully expecting him to be elsewhere, which he generally was, and to leave a message with his secretary. Then, eventually, he would call back.

When Lou Nanne was the GM of the Minnesota North Stars, he always returned the calls. And he always reversed the charges.

He was the only GM in the league to do so, but he had a good reason for it. "The owner told me that if I wanted my office renovated," he said, "I had to come up with the money from somewhere else in my budget. Instead of spending $20,000 returning phone calls from you guys, I made you all pay for the calls and now I've got a lovely office."

• • •

If you ever saw the classic hockey movie *Slapshot*, you'll remember Ogie Oglethorpe, the enforcer of all enforcers. The character was based on a real-life player, Bill "Goldie"

Goldthorpe, who, with his enormous Afro haircut and his threatening glare, not to mention his sledgehammer fists, terrorized the minor leagues for sixteen years.

From 1987 to 1997, Troy Crowder was an NHL version of Ogie Oglethorpe. Crowder was one of the guys at the top of the era's enforcer A-list, along with Bob Probert, Marty McSorley, Tony Twist, John Kordic, and a few others. On any given night, one could beat the other. And the next time they met, there would be a rematch that could easily have a different result.

Crowder, who played mostly for the New Jersey Devils, was a good friend of Mike Hartman, the Buffalo Sabres' enforcer. The two had played junior hockey together in North Bay. At one time, Crowder had played junior hockey in Belleville, and when he got traded, Hartman took over his billet.

One night, when the Sabres were playing the Devils, Crowder scored. This was not, of course, a particularly common occurrence, and later in the game, Hartman congratulated him.

The next time the teams met, Hartman scored. "He'd congratulated me," Crowder said, "so I went over to him and said, 'Nice goal.' He looked at me funny, and the next thing I know, the gloves are flying and we're going at it.

"Because we were such good friends, he knew me and he knew my style. He grabbed my right arm because that was my punching arm, so I had to throw some lefts.

"The chin strap on his helmet had come loose and I swung and missed, but my little finger got hooked into the strap and somehow it got cut.

"So there I am, sitting in the penalty box with Kirk Muller and I told him what had happened. There's blood pouring out of my finger – it took eighteen stitches to close it – and Kirk is laughing away and everybody is wondering what's going on."

Why was Muller laughing?

"I told him what happened," Crowder explained. "At the end of the fight, I said to Hartman, 'What was all that about?' and he said, 'Well you said, "Let's go."'"

"No I didn't," laughed Crowder. "I said, 'Nice goal.'"

• • •

In April 1973, Bob Gainey and I were starting families. Bob's eldest child, Anna, was born and so was my elder son, Andrew. As new parents, we talked about our hopes and aspirations for our children and even joked that a few centuries earlier, we could have had them betrothed on the spot.

Not only were Anna and Andrew never betrothed, they've never even met.

Bob and his wife, Cathy, went on to have three more children, whereas my wife and I had only one more. But the numbers don't matter. You love them all without qualification.

As a parent, one can't help but empathize with Bob Gainey, to sympathize with him, and to understand the heartbreak and anguish that he felt in 2006 when another of his daughters, Laura, was swept overboard from a tall ship about five hundred miles east-southeast of Cape Cod. Her body was never found.

It shouldn't have happened. Laura was in a covered shelter on a rear deck of the ship and dressed for the storm that was raging. She was not new to sailing and even had a tall ship tattooed on her shoulder. It seems logical to assume that any danger from the sea would have been greater at the bow of the ship than at the stern. However, a rogue wave hit and swept Laura overboard.

A lot of other things shouldn't have happened in Laura's life, by far the most important being the loss of her mother.

Cathy Gainey, as the youngest of nineteen children, knew the importance of close families. But a brain tumour took her life in 1995. For the entire Gainey family, but especially for the two youngest daughters, Laura and Colleen, it was a devastating turn of events. Cathy was an exceptionally warm, thoughtful, and kind person. That's not an evaluation clouded by the circumstances. Those who knew her regarded her in that fashion long before she died.

Together, she and Bob formed a salt-of-the-earth couple, small-town people who never acquired the cynical, decadent values so prevalent in the world of professional sports. For two young girls, at such a formative stage of their life, to lose their mother, especially a mother like Cathy, was a traumatic and debilitating experience.

Bob did everything he could, but a father's love, no matter how deep it might be, does not replace a mother's love. And grief affects us all in different ways, few of them beneficial. Life had been difficult for Laura, but she seemed to have surmounted the most treacherous obstacles and was doing something she loved.

No parent should have to endure the loss of a child. Unfortunately, some must do so, but they are never the same afterwards. The pain may ease in time, but it will never go away entirely. There will be times when, inexplicably, the tears will flow. A previously bright day will suddenly become dark.

Bob Gainey is a strong person, known for accepting his lot in life in stoical fashion. But he didn't deserve that. Nobody does. On February 8, 2010, Bob Gainey walked away from hockey. One of the reasons was that he wanted to spend more time with his family.

• • •

One of the most acerbic writers in the history of journalism has to be Dave Molinari of the *Pittsburgh Post-Gazette*. Being a touch on the acerbic side myself, I always used to enjoy sitting beside Molinari at a game. His comments on the play were hilarious.

The old Montreal Forum, for instance, had girders

that blocked the view of some sections of the ice from some of the press-box seats. During the regular season, the home-town and visiting writers were always given seats near centre ice, where the view was unobstructed, but when the all-star game was staged in Montreal in 1993, the press box was overflowing, and Molinari's designated seat was near the blue line. From that location, it was impossible to see the play in the defending team's end of the rink.

"That's all right," said Molinari. "I've always wanted to have the same view of the game as Paul Coffey."

· · ·

Here's another Molinari story: When the Penguins were playing in the Stanley Cup final in Minnesota in 1990, we were hanging around the press room before the game. In those days, you never knew who might have press credentials for the playoffs. It could be a tailor, a caterer, a salesman, or anyone else the league officials wanted to impress.

One of these people walked up to Molinari and said, ever so politely, "Do you mind if I ask you a stupid question?" Molinari looked him up and down and said, without a hint of a smile, "There's ample precedent."

· · ·

There's one Molinari story I heard that I thought might have been apocryphal, but it was witnessed by Tom

MacMillan, who for years covered hockey for the other Pittsburgh paper, the *Tribune Review*, and went on to become the Penguins media-relations director.

The two of them were due to travel somewhere for a game, but a snowstorm hit the Pittsburgh area, and even though they had arrived at the airport in the morning, they were still awaiting their flight in the afternoon. At one point, they had boarded the plane, only to be taken off again and sent back into the airport. The hours dragged on and Molinari was becoming increasingly agitated. He is not a man to suffer in silence, and MacMillan heard all his views on airports, airlines, Pittsburgh weather, and a number of other related subjects.

Totally bedraggled, demoralized, and almost resigned to his fate, Molinari was sitting slumped in the waiting area when a man in a motorized wheelchair passed by. With his gnarled hand, perhaps the only part of his body he could move, he was pushing the joystick that dictated the wheelchair's movement.

Molinari looked at the guy and said, "I know just how you feel."

• • •

For the most part, today's NHL coaches don't worry about curfews. For one thing, fewer nights are spent on the road. In an earlier era, teams would play a game, then leave on a commercial flight the following morning.

Now, they all have charters, and even though league rules require that a visiting team must stay in the building for at least forty-five minutes after a game, it's a rule that is often ignored. Almost without exception, players are in their own beds at home after a road game, or they are in the next city on the road trip.

In the days of commercial flights, players would often go to a bar after the game, then stagger back to the hotel in the wee hours. In the United States, some jurisdictions don't require bars to close until 4:00 a.m. In some states, the bars don't have to close at all.

Even in cities that have earlier closing hours, there are ways to get a drink. In Pennsylvania, for example, bars are required to close at 2:00 a.m. But Pennsylvania also has "private clubs" that conveniently open at 2:00 a.m. and stay open until 8:00 a.m. Even though the clubs are ostensibly "private," memberships can be acquired on the spot.

Another reason that curfews have fallen out of favour is the nature of today's game. With the average annual salary closing in on $2 million, competition for jobs is intense. Players are in better shape than they have ever been, and they take their conditioning seriously.

Showing up for a game with a hangover is no longer considered to be an option.

•   •   •

In the seventies, the Vancouver Canucks could never handle the Canadiens. That was no great surprise. The Canucks had only come into the league in 1970, and by the middle of the decade, the Canadiens were getting another one of their dynasties rolling.

In 1974–75, for instance, the Canadiens' record was 47–14–19 for 113 points. The Canucks' record for that year was 38–32–10: a respectable showing, but nothing close to the Canadiens. When the two teams drew each other in the playoffs, there seemed to be little doubt which team would emerge victorious.

The Canucks' coach was a crusty old veteran named Phil Maloney, who, not unreasonably, quickly tired of the openly disparaging remarks from the media regarding his team's chances. When the Canucks lost the series opener 6–0, he was asked how he felt about his chances now. "We lost one game," growled Maloney. "We weren't expecting to sweep them."

· · ·

When I was at the Montreal *Gazette*, it was a widely held opinion that if Hollywood ever needed someone to play the role of the hard-bitten, hard-working, hard-drinking newspaper editor, Brodie Snider would be their man.

He wouldn't need to act.

In 1973, when I started work at the *Gazette*, Brodie was the assistant sports editor. The sports editor, Ted Blackman, was rarely seen. Blackman would occasionally drop in to bang out a column or to give Brodie advice he didn't need, then disappear to Crescent Street to do some "research" until the wee hours.

As a result, Brodie ran the department. And, as far as the major editorial aspects of the business were concerned, he ran the entire paper.

When a particularly sticky journalistic dilemma arose, Brodie was called in to resolve it.

When there was serious journalistic work to be done, Brodie was called in to do it.

In 1976, for instance, when Montreal hosted the Olympics, almost every available staffer was shipped off to cover an event, often a sport that he or she had never seen before.

Every day, the *Gazette* put out an Olympic supplement that ranged from twenty-four to forty-eight pages. Only two people stayed behind to put together that supplement – and if you don't know journalism, believe me, that's a monumental task, especially when much of the copy was coming from people unfamiliar with their subject matter.

One of the two deskers who handled the massive influx of copy was Brodie. After that, it didn't really matter who the second one was.

But Brodie wasn't only relied upon to handle a heavy load. He was also relied upon to do the best work. In the time I was there, the *Gazette* won a number of National

Newspaper Awards. Every single one, in every category
except photography, had been edited by Brodie. And
although he wasn't directly involved in the creation of the
photographic entries, he did have a hand in determining
which ones should be entered in the competition.

He went on to become sports editor and managing
editor and was, quite simply, the best newspaperman I
ever met.

After work, either in Mother Martin's, the bar adjacent to the *Gazette*, or in the Montreal Press Club – where
"first last call" was usually shouted around 3:00 a.m. – he
was a great deal of fun. In the office, not so much.

He buried his head in his work and rarely spoke, preferring instead to hammer out notes on his old Underwood
typewriter, then fire them across the large communal desk
to whichever staffer was the intended recipient.

Discussions in the sports department office rarely
included Brodie. We were there to get the job done (all
the better to get to Mother Martin's early), and although
conversation was tolerated, if it went on too long, Brodie
made it clear in singularly graphic language that it was
time it was terminated.

And he had no time at all for idle chatter.

One afternoon, Montreal experienced a major thunder-
storm. The heavens opened, and one of the staffers, Bob
Morrissey, got out of his chair, walked over to the window,
and announced, "It's really coming down out there."

"It would be a hell of a story if it was going up, Bob,"

growled Brodie, never lifting his eyes from the copy he was editing.

In one of my previous books, *I Am Not Making This Up*, I included a few stories about life with Brodie. During the writing of this book, on May 24, 2011, to be exact, Brodie died. He was eighty-one, and he was the last of his breed.

• • •

Brodie once told me a story about one of his predecessors as a sports editor in Montreal, Elmer Ferguson. Like Brodie, Ferguson was one of those crusty, dogmatic newspapermen who made his department his empire. Unlike Brodie, Ferguson supplemented his income in a manner that would be unacceptable today but wasn't that uncommon during the Great Depression.

Ferguson became sports editor of the *Montreal Herald* in 1913 and held the post for thirty-nine years. As is the case with every sports editor, he often received requests for preferential treatment from special-interest groups. If the group accommodated Ferguson, he provided accommodation in return – and he prided himself on knowing exactly what price to charge.

A prestigious golf club wanting a picture of its champion to appear in the *Herald* would have to pay a lot more than a small-town figure-skating club would pay to have its picture of choice in the paper.

One day, a man appeared in Ferguson's office clutching a picture of his curling-club champions. He wanted the picture to appear in the newspaper along with a short article describing their achievements. He was prepared to pay for the favour. Ferguson looked the man up and down. He saw the muddy coveralls. He saw the weather-worn boots. He saw the unkempt hair. He made his evaluation. "Twenty-five dollars," he said.

The man reached into his coveralls and pulled out a huge roll of twenties. Ferguson's eyes bulged. "And two hundred for the picture," he quickly added.

Today, when the Professional Hockey Writers Association selects its annual inductee into the media wing of the Hockey Hall of Fame, that person receives the Elmer Ferguson Award.

# CHAPTER SIX

*There is no crueller tyranny than that which is perpe-
trated under the shield of law and in the name of justice.*

Montesquieu

**If you examine the National Hockey League's**
dynasties over the years, you'll find that they have one
thing in common: the hockey decisions were made by
a hockey man.

He may not have been the team's owner. In fact, he
rarely had any share of the team. But when it came to
hockey matters, he had carte blanche.

The first serious NHL dynasty came into being in the
fifties, when the Montreal Canadiens won five Stanley
Cup championships in a row – and coach Toe Blake
always insisted they would have had another had it not
been for poor refereeing. The general manager at the time
was Frank J. Selke.

When Sam Pollock took over from Selke as the
Canadiens' general manager, the team won ten Stanley
Cups in fifteen years.

The Canadiens were displaced by the New York Islanders, who won four consecutive Cups starting in 1980. Then came the Edmonton Oilers of the eighties. The general managers of those teams were Bill Torrey and Glen Sather.

Dynasties aren't as common these days as they once were, but the two teams that have come closest since the Oilers' heyday are the Detroit Red Wings under Ken Holland and the New Jersey Devils under Lou Lamoriello. They won four and three Cups respectively.

In every single case, those men had a free hand to build the team as they saw fit. The lone exception was the 1990 victory by the Oilers. The team won four Cups when Sather had the last word in hockey matters. As the eighties wound down, owner Peter Pocklington increasingly dictated the team's spending. It was no accident that this interference coincided with the Oilers' decline, and their 1990 Cup victory was more of a fortuitous culmination of events than part of a dynasty.

In my book *Why the Leafs Suck and How They Can Be Fixed*, I expanded on the need for a hockey man at the top of a successful organization and put forward the argument that the Leafs' horrible record over four decades was directly attributable to the fact that the team was run by dilettantes and entrepreneurs, but never by true hockey men. Despite their lack of knowledge, those people routinely interfered in hockey matters, with disastrous results.

Now take the idea one step further. Look at the

National Hockey League as a whole. Hockey is its business. The well-being of the league depends on the well-being of the game. But where are the hockey men? Who makes the hockey decisions?

The answer is that the governors – the team owners – decide the direction of the game and for the most part they know nothing about hockey. They're experts in oil drilling, movie renting, pension-plan management, website technology, or some other enterprise. But not hockey.

Their favourite approach is to debate the issues, then turn the matter over to the league's battalion of lawyers for a decision. Granted, they will make a concession every decade or so and allow a hockey man to get involved. The only recent example of this came after the lockout – the one-year shutdown that was the result of decisions made by non-hockey people – when they accepted the recommendations that Colin Campbell had been trying to implement for years.

Campbell, the league's senior vice-president of hockey operations, played in the NHL. He coached in the NHL. He has a son who plays in the NHL. He is a fully quali-fied hockey man.He is assisted by a number of other people who have spent their lives in hockey, most notably Mike Murphy, Jim Gregory, and Kris King. The late E.J. McGuire was also an integral part of the team until his death in early 2011.

The group, which works out of the league's Toronto office, well away from the distractions of the New York head-office aggregation, examines every aspect of the game and figures out ways in which it can be improved. Then Campbell does his best to convince the governors to accept the changes.

The evidence is there if anyone in the NHL is willing to look at it. For the NHL to be more successful, hockey people need to be involved at the highest level and their recommendations need to be implemented.

The lawyers have had their day, and they have made a mess of it.

•   •   •

It was always easy to criticize Colin Campbell. That's probably why so many people in the media did it. It didn't require a lot of thought. It didn't require much insight. You just screamed about his inability to hand out the type of suspension you wanted to see, decreed that he was incompetent, and moved on to your next target.

In fact, Campbell, who stepped down as the league's arbiter of justice on June 1, 2011, after thirteen years on the job, is the primary reason that today's hockey is such a delight.

You might not agree with some of his suspensions, but look at it this way: when it comes to suspensions, could anyone make everyone happy all the time? Another fact to consider is that when these suspensions were made, even though it was Campbell who took centre stage, the decisions were made by a group of hockey lifers, people who know and understand the game.

In recent years, there has been a clamouring for a firmer hand on that front and Campbell has provided it. When he suspended Matt Cooke of the Pittsburgh Penguins for the final ten games of the regular season and the first round of the 2011 playoffs, he far exceeded what was the precedent for such infractions. In effect, he gave Cooke a suspension that lasted until October, because the Penguins didn't survive the first round.

The point that most people miss is that Campbell's responsibilities extended far beyond discipline. In today's game, for the first time in most fans' memory, the elite players are allowed to exhibit their magnificent skills. It is Campbell who spearheaded the move to get rid of the clutching and grabbing that had made the game tedious.

His predecessor, Brian Burke, had allowed the NHL game to evolve into rugby on ice, one in which any lead was almost insurmountable because scoring chances were so rare.

In the seven-game 2004 Stanley Cup final between the Calgary Flames and the Tampa Bay Lightning, for instance, there were no lead changes. Not a single one in seven games!

In 2003, Campbell started his battle to change the game. He made a number of proposals, but at the time, the NHL Players' Association was preparing for war with the NHL, a war that led to the loss of the 2004–05 season. Just on principle – the principle being that they hadn't been consulted in advance – the PA refused to sanction the changes.

Campbell's approach to refereeing opened up the game and allowed the stars to play as stars. Mario Lemieux had complained about the league's willingness to cater to the game's plumbers, calling it "a garage league." Other stars had complained just as vociferously in private but, lacking Lemieux's status within the game, hadn't gone public.

When the league returned to action after the lockout, Campbell's proposed changes had been collectively bargained and were implemented. The centre red line was eliminated as a factor in two-line passes, thereby allowing the breakaway passes that are now a constant threat. A peripheral result has been an increase in the number of penalty shots – which fans love – because when a breakaway pass works, a defender will sometimes feel the need to haul down the puck-carrier from behind.

Teams that ice the puck were no longer allowed to make substitutions. Under Burke's regime, a tired team under pressure would simply ice the puck and send out fresh players. Now, the tired players stay out, and only the coach's use of the one time out he is allocated each game can give his team the rest it wants.

The tag-up rule came back in. As a result, many offside calls were eliminated. Players already in the offensive zone when the puck crossed the blue line had to come out, but once they were all out, they could go right back in – with the play still alive.

If the puck was behind the goal line, goaltenders were allowed to play it only within the trapezoid-shaped area right behind the net. This eliminated the tedious sight of a team trying to mount an attack by dumping the puck into the corner only to have a goaltender skate over and dump it right back out. Additionally, the size of goaltender equipment was reduced by 11 per cent.

If the game remained tied after five minutes of overtime, a shootout would determine the winner.

Not all of these are Campbell's ideas. But they were all instituted at Campbell's urging. He changed the face of hockey, and he changed it for the better. Much better. Unfortunately, too many people didn't consider that fact when they decided that they didn't like the length of his most recent suspension.

•   •   •

Now, Brendan Shanahan will dispense justice.

"I can't promise you how I will view each individual situation," he said at his first post-appointment press conference. "I do love the physical aspect of hockey and it is a very difficult and fine balance to keep that in the game to allow players to play on their toes, but at the same time know what they can and cannot do.

"If I feel all the criteria of a player trying to injure another player has been met, then I am going to have to act. I can't promise you what was once a three [game suspension] is now a seven. I will promise you when I do make these decisions, I will try and make my thought process, and everything that went into that thought process, very clear and very visible to the hockey world."

Shanahan is a man of integrity and no doubt he means exactly what he says. But walking into that job is like walking into quicksand. No matter how good your intentions might be, there is no firm footing.

●   ●   ●

A perfect example of the problems that are created when decisions are made without the input of hockey people is on display in every single NHL game, in the composite sticks used by the players. Without the slightest thought, let alone careful consideration, the NHL allowed those composite sticks to be introduced, just as years ago, also without due consideration, it allowed aluminum sticks to be introduced.

It was a great irony that one week after Sher-Wood, the world's leading hockey-stick manufacturer, announced it would no longer make wooden sticks due to a lack of demand, Al MacInnis was inducted into the Hockey Hall of Fame.

In his playing days, which probably would have continued well beyond his 2007 induction were it not for an eye injury, MacInnis consistently had the hardest shot in hockey. And he always used a wooden stick.

Once in a while, somebody might whack one harder than MacInnis, but year in, year out, MacInnis had the hardest shot. Before him, Doug Wilson, now general manager of the San Jose Sharks, held the honour. He, too, used nothing but wooden sticks.

Both men won the Norris Trophy as the NHL's best defenceman – Wilson in 1982 and MacInnis in 1999 – and each is convinced that the composite sticks do nothing for the game. In fact, they feel that the introduction of composite sticks is a significant factor in the reduction in scoring.

The problem is that while composite sticks produce blazing shots, they are decidedly inferior to wooden sticks when it comes to the game's finer points. Pucks do indeed fly off a composite stick when you're unleashing a shot. Unfortunately, pucks also fly off them when you're trying to receive a pass. Or even when you're trying to stick-handle. "When I'm at the point and the puck comes to me, I have to know it's there," said MacInnis. "I can't be looking down to see where it got to."

In today's game, where every player skates like the wind, you can't take even a split second to look down. If you do, the checker will be on you and the shooting lane will have disappeared. That's one of the reasons why there are so many blocked shots today.

MacInnis was devastating as a power-play quarter-back, and one of the reasons was that he was a master at letting a shot go in a hurry or, if a checker was coming at

him, making a quick pass to an open teammate. He could
do it because with his wooden stick, he knew where the
puck was without having to look. When he originally
took possession, he saw the puck coming and felt it hit his
stick; that was enough. That's not the case with a composite stick.

"There's also another factor," said Wilson, who was as
great a skater as he was a shooter and was therefore the
man who carried the puck up on the power play. "When
you're a defenceman, you tend to push the puck a lot
when you're carrying it. You don't stick-handle like a
forward. With the composite sticks, you can't control the
puck as well when you try to push it." If you're battling to
control the puck, you'll probably fall prey to checkers
who are harassing you as you move up the ice. Therefore,
the attack will be stopped before it gets started and another
potential scoring opportunity will have been wasted.

And Wayne Gretzky, a guy who knows a bit about
scoring, wishes composite sticks would be banned. "I think
every coach in the league feels the same way," he said.
Coaches don't say much publicly because they don't want
to suggest that their entire team needs help in the way it
handles the puck. But they see the deficiencies every day.

Supporters of composite sticks say that they give ordinary players a tremendous shot. And that's true. But where
is that shot going? If it's on the net, it may well be 20 mph
faster than its counterpart from a wooden stick and may
therefore beat a goalie when another shot wouldn't. But

composite sticks are nowhere near as accurate as wooden sticks, so any gain from speed is negated by the lack of accuracy.

How often have you seen a player fire away from twenty feet out and miss the net? Still, players love to have booming shots, and, for most of them, the only way to get one is to have a composite stick.

Naturally, the stick manufacturers promote their use among the pros. A decent wooden stick sells for one-tenth of the price of a top-end composite stick – roughly $30 compared to $300. For a beer-league player, this may not be a matter for concern. If he's using the same stick as his favourite pro, he'll justify the expense. But it's a devastating development to many kids who want to play the game.

We all know what peer pressure is like among kids. If a few players on a team have composite sticks, the others want them as well, even though their parents may not be able to afford them. How many potential NHL stars will never develop because they chose to play soccer or some other less expensive sport rather than put up with the perceived shame of having an inferior stick?

Talk to hockey people about the composite-stick problem and they say it's too late. As Sher-Wood's decision indicates, the composite sticks are now so ingrained in the game, they're all but universal.

But need they be?

Baseball doesn't allow aluminum bats because they change the nature of the game. A quality pitcher will break a bat with an inside pitch, whereas if the batter is using an aluminum bat, the pitch will probably become a hit down the line. Recognizing this, major league baseball insisted that all bats be made of wood – and only wood, Sammy Sosa notwithstanding.

Golfers can't use just any clubs they want. They have to conform to Professional Golf Association standards. Clubs do evolve – witness the big heads on modern drivers – but the governing body makes sure that no unreasonable advantage accrues. Even the nature of the grooves on the club face is controlled.

Had the NHL been run by hockey people instead of lawyers, the potential changes being wrought by composite sticks might have been foreseen. But unfortunately, the foresight of the NHL's movers and shakers rarely extends past deciding where to go for dinner. Then, when they finally reach agreement and get to the appointed establishment, they'll sit around sipping their aperitifs and bemoaning the lack of scoring in their game.

•   •   •

Towards the end of his career, Mario Lemieux, like Wayne Gretzky before him, turned his attention to being more of a setup man than a scorer. "The last few years I have been more of a passer than a shooter," Lemieux said during the World Cup in 2004. "My one-on-one game is not what it used to be. I'm trying to be patient with the puck and set up the other guys a little bit better. My game has changed over the years."

But his stick didn't change. He still used a wooden stick even though most players had switched to composites. "I've tried the other sticks, even this summer," Lemieux said, "and I just can't get used to them. My shooting is not accurate. I tried them a couple of times this summer and I was shooting in the corners. I just don't like the feel of them. I can't feel the puck, and my game is feeling the puck."

Two of the greatest scorers in the history of the game – Mario Lemieux and Wayne Gretzky – both refused to use composite sticks because the sticks simply were not good enough. Composites prevented the players from exhibiting the magnificent skills that they possessed.

But the NHL allowed composite sticks anyway, and in 2010, the last manufacturer of wooden sticks shut down its operation.

# CHAPTER SEVEN

*"What will happen when all this is over? Have you thought of that?"*

*"I shall be older, alone and have memories of a glorious time when I was happy and loved, even if it could not be mine forever. I shall have had laughter, imagination and friendship and I shall keep my memories without bitterness."*

Anne Perry, *The Hyde Park Headsman*

**Sam Pollock always believed** that December was not a good month to sell hockey tickets. As a result, the legendary general manager of the Montreal Canadiens always arranged for the team to take a long western road trip in December.

I was covering the Canadiens for the Montreal *Gazette* at the time, and when we went on that extended run, we would be gone anywhere from ten days to two weeks. Much to my wife's displeasure, Montreal would experience a blizzard while we were away, but it's hard to overly concern oneself with such things when one is relaxing in a western resort.

The trip would usually start with games in St. Louis and Chicago. Then we'd head west for an in-season vacation of five days or so. One year, we went to Squaw Valley. A couple of times, we went to a resort in Colorado Springs. On other occasions, it was a resort on the west coast of California just north of Los Angeles.

After that, refreshed and rejuvenated, the Canadiens would make a west-coast swing: Oakland (the Seals were part of the league in those days), Los Angeles, and Vancouver. The message to the Canadiens was always clear: If you like these all-expenses-paid breaks at fancy resorts, you'd better show it in your play.

During Scott Bowman's tenure as coach of the Canadiens, they played more than fifty games on those west-coast swings. They lost two.

• • •

The year we were in Squaw Valley, I decided to try skiing, something I'd never done before. The players weren't allowed to go, and the three guys covering for the French-language newspapers still had to fill their three pages every day, whether the team was playing or not, so they weren't available. That left Red Fisher as a possible companion on the slopes.

I went skiing by myself.

All the people I had talked to had said, "You'll catch on to it. You can skate, so you'll be able to ski. It's not that much different." Of course, all the people I had talked to just happened to be gifted athletes and not overweight and decidedly unfit journalists, a fact I should perhaps have considered before I set out on my quest.

However, I rented some equipment and headed off towards the nearest gondola, hastily coming to the conclusion that I had been well advised. Getting along the trail from the rental shack to the gondola wasn't at all difficult. Perhaps that would change once I put the skis on, but we'd worry about that stage when we got to it.

The gondola ride seemed interminable, but the other skiers were talking about the great skiing conditions and how much fun they were having, so the wait just heightened the anticipation.

When the gondola reached the top and we all poured out, I put on the skis.

This was prior to the era of step-in bindings. Levers had to be pushed and clips had to be attached. Already, this was getting to be a bit more difficult than I had expected. There were no levers or clips on skates.

It was already too late to do the smart thing. But even with that concession in mind, it would still have made a lot of sense to head downhill right then. Instead, I headed for a nearby chairlift. My memory says this run was called "Suicide." But the mind plays tricks. Looking at a map of the Squaw Valley Mountain these days, it was either the Mainline or the Newport, both of which commence at the top of the mountain. Perhaps the name has been changed. Or perhaps I just gave the run a name that seemed appropriate.

The mountain wasn't busy, and there wasn't a line for the chairlift – which would have sent a message to anyone with half a brain – but as skiers arrived, I watched them getting on the chairlift to see how they did it. It didn't appear to be that difficult so, after a while, I gave it a try. Astonishingly, I made it.

A problem loomed on the horizon, however. I had watched people get on. I had no idea how they got off.

For those of you who haven't skied, when the lift gets to the disembarking point, you simply slide forward off the chair. You're at the top of a small slope, so you ski down it and you're on your way. But from my vantage point of a climbing chairlift, all I could see was a chair reaching the top with a skier or two on it, then making a turn and starting back downhill with no skiers.

At that location, there was a little shack with a platform beside it. So when my chair got there, I jumped sideways onto the platform, went head over heels, and ended up with my back against the railing and my skis in the air.

This prompted a pretty young girl to emerge from the shack and, stifling a chuckle, ask me if I was all right. She had stopped the lift, thereby saving me from being hit in the head by the next chair. "Have you ever skied before?" she asked.

"Well, no. But I've skated."

She explained how to get onto the slope, then said, "Perhaps you shouldn't have come on this run. Be careful." Of course. But as a seasoned skater, I'd be in good shape. Off I went.

To say that I skied down would be something of an exaggeration. I side-stepped part of the way. It seemed to be the thing to do since at some points the slope was so steep that I could touch the side of it with one hand.

I rolled part of the way. Occasionally, I glided a few feet here and there before falling down. By the time the sun was beginning to set, I had worked my way back to the upper gondola station.

By now, being a veteran of the slopes, I felt confident enough to glide towards it with a bit of speed. Actually, it was more than a bit of speed. It was too much speed, and suddenly, I was past the station and heading downhill.

At the thought of having to "ski" all the way to the bottom, panic set in so I executed a skating stop – I put the two skis parallel and dug them into the snow. It worked. I stopped. I also went head over heels and ended up on my back in a little V-shaped drainage ditch.

The good news was that there was no water in the ditch. The bad news was that I was stranded like Gregor Samsa, the character in Franz Kafka's *The Metamorphosis*, who woke up one morning and found himself turned into a giant beetle-like insect.

I was lying on my back with my skis dug into the snow and sticking straight up.

I tried to bend forward to pop the skis, but because of the bulky clothing and perhaps, it must be said, a certain amount of inflexibility, I couldn't reach them. I tried to turn my body, but the skis wouldn't let me. People skied by and grinned. Others ignored me.

By now, there was hardly anyone left on the hill. The sun was going down. I tried to remember the Kafka story and wondered if Gregor Samsa died of starvation while stuck on his back.

Suddenly there was a whooshing of skis and a Ski Patrol guy was standing beside me. "Do you need help?" he asked.

"Well, perhaps a bit."

He popped the skis, and I walked back to the gondola.

That evening, the guys were wondering where I had been all afternoon. "I was out skiing," I said. "I went right to the top of the mountain. If you can skate, you know, skiing is a walk in the park."

•  •  •

Like most professional athletes, hockey players tend to be superstitious. They leave the dressing room in a specific order, they follow a well-established ritual in the pre-game skate, and they often base their choice of street clothes on recent success – or lack of it.

And they grow playoff beards.

This last one always seemed to me to be a waste of time. Adam Oates, an excellent player who was also a graduate of the highly regarded Rensselaer Polytechnic Institute, refused to do it. His mathematically inclined mind led him to the observation that of the sixteen teams taking part in the NHL's post-season activities, only one wins the Stanley Cup. Therefore, Oates noted, the chances of the playoff beard making a meaningful contribution are only a little more than 6 per cent, a rather poor success rate.

The practice began with the New York Islanders in the early eighties, an era in which teams were required to open the playoffs with four games in five nights. Since free time was so scarce during that hectic stretch, some players decided to skip shaving.

Because the Islanders were on their way to winning four consecutive Stanley Cups, the beards were interpreted as a contributor to success, and they stayed.

Now, almost every player grows a beard in the post-season, even though the Islanders' immediate successor as the reigning NHL dynasty, the Edmonton Oilers, eschewed the practice. The accepted version of the reasoning behind their decision is that Wayne Gretzky couldn't grow a respectable beard, and in order to spare him the embarrassment of displaying scraggly facial hair, the whole team decided against playoff beards.

A similar decision should probably have been made

by the Pittsburgh Penguins in 2009 and 2010 when they were led by Sidney Crosby.

Nevertheless, the practice has even spread to other sports and other levels. Football and basketball teams have been known to do it, as have a number of college teams.

My own opinion is that it hurts hockey's image. The Stanley Cup playoffs are the time of year when interest increases. Fans who may not have seen many hockey games – if any – get caught up in the excitement and want to get to recognize the players. But they can't do it because the beards hide their faces.

Also, hockey likes to promote its reputation as a demanding sport played by some of the toughest and best-conditioned athletes in the world. The game's devotees tell prospective fans about the league's macho image. But how do they reconcile that with Scott Niedermayer winning the Conn Smythe Trophy in 2007 as the best player in the playoffs while sporting a hideous grey beard? Obviously, as Oates irrefutably pointed out, there is no correlation between success and facial hair.

And to expand on his point, if every team does it and only one team wins, there are a lot more losers with beards than winners with beards. So really, the beard should be looked upon as a jinx.

It's a superstition that should be laid to rest.

•  •  •

Tom Martin didn't play a full season in the NHL, but even so, when hockey people get together and start swapping stories, his name often comes up.

He was what Don Cherry would refer to as "a good western Canadian boy" from Victoria, B.C., and a decent junior player. But when the Seattle Breakers added him to their reserve list in 1982, he decided to go to university instead.

He wasn't opposed to playing junior hockey, but he didn't want to play in Seattle, so he let the Victoria Cougars know that if they were to trade for his rights, he would play for them.

Not long before that, the Spokane Flyers had gone bankrupt and the Cougars had purchased the defunct franchise's team bus for a song. But as so many Canadians learn, the transfer of a vehicle across a border that supposedly has free trade in automotive material is not as easy as it seems. Nor is it cheap. As a result, the bus remained in storage in the United States.

Fortuitously, the Breakers just happened to be in need of a bus, so the idea was floated of trading Tom Martin's rights plus $35,000 for the bus.

The deal worked for both sides and was consummated.

For the rest of his career, which included ninety-two games in the NHL, Martin had the nickname of "Bussy." He always took his status as the only player ever to be traded for a bus in good humour, even though he never saw the bus in question. "I know it had bunks on it, and it was definitely team-oriented," he said. "In the Western Hockey League, they travel a lot, and they need a good bus. Maybe it had better wheels than I did."

•   •   •

A *Sports Illustrated* survey a few years ago revealed that half of all Olympic athletes would be willing to take a drug that would eventually prove fatal if that drug allowed them to win their event for five consecutive years.

The basic question is this: How much is it worth to win? It's a question that could be put in hockey terms.

If you were a general manager, would you make a trade to win the Stanley Cup if it meant that your team subsequently spent decades in hockey's wasteland?

It's easy to say that you would. The glory of hoisting the Stanley Cup lasts forever. The team's name will go down in history, whereas a stretch as an also-ran will quickly be forgotten once the team returns to respectability.

But on the other hand, what will the period of decline mean to the team's long-term status? If the team is in the United States, especially the southern United States, it could conceivably be forced to move because of a lack of support. What will the Cup matter then? How many people today care that the Montreal Maroons won a couple of Stanley Cups? The team played its last NHL game in 1938.

There is also another truth that doesn't get mentioned publicly. As far as some general managers are concerned, it's better to be a continual runner-up than a one-time winner. If you're close every year, fans keep coming back. Hope springs eternal. And you keep your job. But once you win, fans expect you to win again. If you don't, they have a tendency to spend their sports dollars elsewhere. When a team's fans disappear, its general manager tends to follow a similar fate.

If you want to debate a specific case rather than generalities, consider the deal Brian Burke, then GM of the Anaheim Ducks, made to acquire Chris Pronger in 2006. To get Pronger, Burke gave up Joffrey Lupul, Ladislav Smid, the Ducks' first-round draft pick in 2007, a conditional 2007 first-round pick, and the second-round pick in 2008.

That's a lot for one player, but Burke already had Scott Niedermayer in place. The Pronger acquisition gave the Ducks the kind of defensive tandem that is rarely seen in today's hockey. It was reminiscent of Gary Suter and Al MacInnis on the blue line of the Calgary Flames when they were one of the dominant teams in the league.

Detractors of the deal wondered out loud why Burke chose this approach. If he wanted to create a top-notch defensive tandem, why didn't he just buy Zdeno Chara?

There's very little to choose between Pronger and Chara – except for the fact that Chara is about three years younger and considerably less injury-prone.

Only days before Burke acquired Pronger, Chara went to the Boston Bruins as an unconditional free agent for a contract that guaranteed him $7.5 million a year for five years. At the time, Pronger had four years left on a contract paying $6.25 million annually.

So if Burke had signed Chara, he could have had the kind of blue-line tandem he coveted, but he wouldn't have had to give away Lupul, Smid, and all those draft picks. All he would have had to do was bump his payroll by $1.25 million to cover the difference between Pronger's salary and Chara's.

Perhaps because Burke had inherited a team that Bryan Murray had stacked with excellent young talent, he felt that he could afford to part with some of it. Whatever the reasoning, the move paid big-time dividends. With Pronger and Niedermayer leading the way, the Ducks won the Stanley Cup in 2007.

As for the fallout of giving away five players for one, Burke didn't have to worry. He skipped out on the Ducks a few months after they won the Cup.

They have won one playoff round since.

•  •  •

More often than not, goaltending makes the difference in the playoffs.

The next most important factor is the defence corps. Give a team a pair of high-quality defencemen and a coach who knows how to use them and they'll be tough to beat.

Having Suter and MacInnis on the blue line was a key factor in the Flames' Stanley Cup victory in 1989. The Colorado Avalanche won the 2001 Cup when Raymond Bourque was added to a team that already had Rob Blake. In 2010, Duncan Keith and Brent Seabrook led the Chicago Blackhawks to the Cup.

But perhaps the best example of a pair of defencemen determining the outcome of a series came in 2002, when the Detroit Red Wings beat the Carolina Hurricanes.

Detroit coach Scott Bowman had two highly lauded veterans at his disposal – Chris Chelios and Nick Lidstrom – but only occasionally were both of them on the ice at the same time. However, at least one of them was on the ice all the time.

Well, not exactly all the time. The series went five games, and for one forty-five-second stint – when Chelios was in the penalty box – neither Lidstrom nor Chelios was available.

During that forty-five-second stretch, the Hurricanes were dominant. They had the Wings bottled up in their own zone and under heavy pressure.

But then Chelios came out of the box and order was resumed.

By virtue of his brilliant use of the TV time outs, Bowman was able to make sure that he could always get one of his two star defencemen on the ice, and that neither was unduly fatigued.

If either a two-minute TV time out or the end of a

period loomed, Bowman would send out both of them.

The Hurricanes were never able to mount sufficient offence to prevent the Wings from winning the Cup.

•  •  •

Mark Messier was never one of those players who lived to be at the rink. In games, he was as intense as anyone, but he wasn't a great fan of practice, and he absolutely loathed training camp.

It was no accident that more often than not, Messier found a way to miss training camp, be it through a contract dispute, an "injury," or time owed because of international commitments. If there had been a Canada Cup tournament in late summer, those who participated could take time off from training camp. Messier took every available second.

When the Oilers got stuck with that league-mandated goodwill trip in September 1990, it seemed to them that the players had hardly managed to find time to take the Stanley Cup on its annual tour before the season started again.

In fact, the situation wasn't as bad as it could be: the Oilers won the Cup on May 24, 1990. As the decade ground on, NHL commissioner Gary Bettman extended the season further and further so that by the time the Dallas Stars won the Cup in 1999, they did so on June 19. And it could have gone longer. That was only Game 6.

But in September 1990, the Oilers found themselves in Germany getting ready for another season. Not one of them had done any serious training since the Cup had been lifted, and here they were, playing in a round-robin tournament for the less-than-coveted Epson Cup against the St. Louis Blues and the local Düsseldorf team from the German league.

The arena wasn't even enclosed. Girders rose from the stands to hold up a roof that protected fans from the elements, but there was no wall between the edge of the roof and the last row of seats. On the day the Oilers were to play, there was fog on the ice.

Coach John Muckler took the game a little more seriously than Messier did – which wasn't hard. In fact, Muckler, looking at it from the point of view of NHL bragging rights on the international stage, took it quite seriously. Messier couldn't wait for it to be over.

Prior to the game, Muckler walked into the dressing room, got the attention of his assembled players, and started to make a little speech. "This is a must-win game," he began. Messier's head shot up. So did his eyebrows. "Wha-a-a-t?" he shouted.

No one else could have got away with that. Muckler was an old-line coach, and while he was no dictator, he still demanded that as coach, his pronouncements were not to be questioned.

But Messier was right. This was the Oilers' first game since May 24, the night of another must-win game, in

Muckler's view. On that occasion, Muckler was right. He didn't want his team facing the coin flip of a seventh game. He wanted them instead to win the Stanley Cup that night – which they did.

A pre-season frolic in Düsseldorf against a third-rate team on a foggy, open-air patch of ice in September was not a must-win game.

Muckler paused. He saw Messier's point and allowed that as long as the Oilers put out a decent effort, it would be good enough. It was. The Oilers played at something less than their highest level, but they still won.

•   •   •

Pat Burns and I didn't always see eye to eye. Not that it mattered much.

Pat was the kind of person who could get mad at you, then go for a beer with you. Like many of the best hockey coaches, when he was at work, he was a professional grump. You wouldn't see him sharing a joke with the players or taking part in one of their elaborate practical jokes. He'd curse them to their faces, but if they ever got into any trouble, he'd be the first one there to help them out.

After the memorial service for Burns on November 29, 2010, Martin Brodeur, who is the total opposite of a professional grump, recalled a story that perfectly summed up the way that Pat Burns treated his players.

Brodeur recalled an occasion when he and Burns were having a chat in the coach's office, relaxing before a game. It was the kind of thing Brodeur would do. Some goalies say they can't talk to the media on the day of the game, but Marty would talk during TV time outs if they'd let him.

After a while, Burns said, "You should go and sit in the room. I have to go in there and blow a fuse now."

He was, of course, referring to the dressing room. As Don Cherry likes to point out, it's not a locker room. Hockey dressing rooms don't have lockers, they have stalls. And when hockey people are talking about that place, it's always just "the room."

Brodeur went on his way and got comfortably settled in before Burns arrived. Then the tirade began. Burns screamed. He broke sticks. He pounded the table. He berated the players. He turned purple. He yelled some more. Then he stormed out.

"I was just shaking my head," said Brodeur. "I was trying not to laugh, and thinking, 'Man, he's got it all figured out.'

"We won the Cup that year."

•    •    •

The only major source of disagreement between Pat Burns and myself had to do with the style of play he demanded.

In other areas – the importance of the game's heritage, the incompetence of the people in the NHL's New York office, and even such issues as the role of the police in today's society and the unfortunate developments on the political front – we were always in agreement.

We both wanted hockey to work in the United States, but it was my feeling that as long as the game catered to coaches like Burns, Roger Neilson, Jacques Lemaire, and a few others, it was going to have trouble doing so. They were the defensive coaches, the people who insisted that defence had to be paramount from the start of the game to its finish.

It was Burns's point – and one that couldn't be denied – that in order for him to stay employed, his team had to win games. And with the rules being the way they were, it made sense to stress defence.

I agreed with that. My complaint was mostly with the people who made the rules, the people who saw nothing wrong with the clutching and grabbing that went on in those days, the people who couldn't understand that if the game were to be successful, the highly skilled players had to be able to exhibit those skills.

If they did understand the problems, they were too dense to do anything about them.

Defence is fine if you've got a sophisticated fan base. In those markets, fans can watch a defensive game and love it. But if you've got an unsophisticated fan base, which was certainly the case in many of the American markets that the NHL was trying to crack, then you needed a greater emphasis on offence.

Since my complaint was mostly with the person in the New York office who was primarily responsible for determining the nature and style of the game – who happened to be Brian Burke at that time – it was somewhat unfair of me to blame Burns for the kind of game his Toronto Maple Leafs were playing.

Nevertheless, I complained in print that because of Burns's edicts, the Leafs played a boring game and seemed more concerned with putting the puck behind the net than in it.

He didn't like that and let me know it. But once he'd made his point, it was over. We were friends again.

•   •   •

The game that Burns liked his team to play was invariably one of defence first. Only after defensive duties were fully under control could a player think about offence. And even then, whether Burns liked my saying it or not, there was definitely a priority on getting the puck behind the opponent's net. While it was there, you weren't going to give up any goals. You could try to generate an offence back there, and even though it might be difficult to do so, at least it wouldn't backfire. If the puck was behind the opponents' net, they wouldn't be breaking out with speed on your outnumbered defence.

In their own end, the Leafs had strict responsibilities. The left-winger was responsible for the opponent's right point. The right-winger was responsible for the left point. The defencemen were responsible for the area in front of the net.

The centre? Well, he was the key to Pat's system. He had to read and react. Not only was he free to go all over the defensive zone, it was mandatory that he did so.

That's why Burns and Doug Gilmour got along so well; Gilmour was a master at this. He was a superb defensive player who was agile, intelligent, and offensively dangerous. He could make the transition from superb defensive centre to scoring threat in milliseconds.

He fit perfectly into Burns's system and Burns knew it. As he liked to say, "My system is pretty simple. The wingers and defencemen are responsible for specific areas. The centre is busier than a one-legged man in an ass-kicking contest."

## CHAPTER EIGHT

*Everything makes sense, Harry. It's just that sometimes, it
takes a while to figure out what the sense is.*

Robert Goddard, *Never Go Back*

**To the National Hockey League,** size matters.

So even though neither move is imminent, you can
expect at least two things in the NHL to get bigger in the
near future – the nets and the league itself.

Let's start with the league. Thus far, the only way
commissioner Gary Bettman has been able to increase
revenues appreciably has been through expansion. His
American network television strategy over the years has
been a disaster, his marketing of the league has been ordinary at best, and his decision to kill the 2004–05 season
certainly did nothing to increase revenues.

Even though the league agreed to a new $2 billion TV
deal in the spring of 2011, it remains to be seen whether
this was a good deal or a bad one. Certainly the money
sounds impressive. But the deal covered every conceivable
form of transmittable images for the subsequent ten years,

and because of the way the internet is being used for more and more applications, this may prove to be a low price.

In another area, it has to be conceded that the subsequent imposition of the salary cap put more money into the rich owners' pockets by limiting their spending on payrolls. But it was their own money they were saving.

Even though revenues have gradually gone up since the lockout, there is a simple reason for that. The financial burden has been transferred to the fans. Ticket prices have risen appreciably across the board, and Bettman's mid-lockout refrain of "We're doing it for the fans" now brings nothing more than sardonic laughter. In addition to increasing ticket prices across the board, more and more teams have introduced the "premium ticket" concept. This means that if the local team is facing a team you'd like to see, prices are escalated accordingly.

They've also added "administrative fees" and seat licences. But even owners admit that there is a limit to the gouging they can inflict on the fans and that they're probably as close to that limit as they care to go.

So in a frantic attempt to justify his continued employment, Bettman will almost certainly fall back upon his tried-and-true concept of selling franchises to unsuspecting investors and sharing the profit among the existing investors.

In my opinion, the cynical among us might suggest that this approach comes perilously close to being a Ponzi scheme, but that's probably pushing it a bit. Either way, for a mathematician, thirty-two is a much more attractive number than the current thirty. It creates a nice balance – sixteen teams make the playoffs and sixteen don't.

Furthermore, the rumours of a realignment of the NHL into four divisions simply won't go away, even though the league denies them. A league with four eight-team divisions is almost certainly the way of the future.

If Bettman can get $300 million for an expansion team, and he can sell two of them, each of the existing owners gets $20 million. The players, of course, get nothing.

There's ample precedent in the NHL for this kind of thing. When big money is waved in front of the owners, it gets snapped up with little regard for the consequences.

•  •  •

As for the size of the nets in the National Hockey League, if you read between the lines of some of the statements that are repeatedly made by hockey executives, you know what's coming.

The league readily admits that the game needs more scoring. Bettman admits it nearly every time he has a major press conference. Furthermore, it's no secret that the league has given the matter of larger nets serious consideration. In fact, the larger nets have been tried out and exhibited as part of think tanks to which the media were invited as observers.

Even though some great hockey thinkers and purists

are appalled by the concept, there's just too much of an undercurrent in the league at the moment to think that the larger nets are not the way of the future.

And really, what else can the league do? The players have accepted the new officiating standard that was imposed after the lockout, and still, scoring hasn't increased.

The idea was that once the league got rid of clutching and grabbing, the skilled players would blossom. In many ways, they have. The games are now much more exciting. But the goalies have risen to the occasion and the free-flow game hasn't produced any marked increase in scoring.

Blocked shots are a way of life now, with even the wimpiest player expected to do it as a matter of course, and since the league insists that it can't think of a way to reduce the size of goaltenders' equipment to a sensible level, where else can they go?

A number of types of new nets have been proposed, some that have posts that curve outwards, some that are radically larger and some that are higher but not wider. The variation that seems the most popular adds eight inches to the standard six-foot width and six inches to the standard four-foot height.

When you sit in the stands and see these nets in place, they don't look any larger than the ones currently in use. But that small increase is significant in that it provides an extra six square feet for the snipers to shoot at.

It's those extra eight inches in width that will have the biggest effect on the game. The extra height will have

some impact, but the extra width is a much more important factor. It means that goalies will no longer be able to
flop down into a butterfly position and cover the entire
lower quarter of the net without exposing their five-hole.

Goalies have been getting taller over the years, and,
like players at other positions, they have become more
proficient. But they've also learned how to make themselves more efficient with the minimum of work. If they
drop down, they don't need to see the puck or make any
further moves. Their leg pads are the maximum width the
league allows, and they therefore leave no low opening
even though their knees may be more than a foot apart.
The lower portion of the net is covered from post to post.
This forces an attacking player to shoot high, but not too
high. That's no easy feat if you're on the edge of the crease.

But with the wider nets, goalies will be forced to
move. If they merely drop down and expose those extra
inches inside the post, the shooters will soon learn to take
advantage – as they did in the days before the size of goalie
equipment reached its present ridiculous dimensions.
Goalies will have to move to the puck, and once they
move to one post, they'll create a larger opening at the
other post, which the accurate shooters will exploit.

When the subject of larger nets comes up, a number
of arguments are made by those who want the nets left as
they are. Some say that if the nets are made larger, hockey
will become like basketball, with too much scoring.

That would be true if the proposed enlargement were

considerable. But an extra eight inches in width and six inches in height is so negligible that the average fan wouldn't notice the difference. These are not soccer nets that are being proposed. It will still require a great deal of skill to beat an NHL goalie – but it will happen more often than is the case today.

The best way to increase scoring, many fans say, is to reduce the size of goalie equipment.

Of course it is. But the NHL is a league run by lawyers, and they can't figure out a way to do it while following the tenets they learned in law school. To them, any new rule has to be "fair" and "just" and everybody has to be "equal under the law." Those of us fortunate enough to have escaped the legal profession would just say to the goalies, "We're going to measure your chest, waist, arms, and hips when you're wearing Kevlar protection that the police use to stop bullets. And that, sir, is the maximum you're allowed. As for leg pads, widths are ten inches, but you can add some limited protection to the back of your leg if you want. If you don't like it, the Russian league is always looking for goalies."

But that's far too simple for lawyers.

The larger nets will demand more from goalies and at the same time reward skilled offensive players. Surely, that's what fans want.

And in the not-too-distant future, that's what they'll get.

· · ·

A favourite prank in hockey circles – or anywhere else that young men gather for that matter – is bed-moving.

During my days in the military, we had a guy who was such a sound sleeper that we took his bed, moved it out of the door of the barracks, set it out on the road, and festooned it with toilet paper. That may not sound like a particularly innovative prank, but we were proud of ourselves. After all, the bed's owner was asleep in the bed at the time.

One of the NHL's best bed-moving stories involves Jeremy Roenick, who was an irrepressible prankster.

He didn't just move Ryan Clowe's bed, he moved his entire hotel room and set it up beside the elevator.

The bedside tables were there. The telephone. The lamps. The chests of drawers. The stuff that passes for art in hotel rooms. Everything.

When Clowe stepped out of the elevator, he came face to face with his entire room, set up in identical fashion to the one he had left. He knew it was his because of the personal items on the bedside tables. But this time, the room and its furnishings were no longer behind a locked door. They were in the alcove beside the elevator.

Clowe was so impressed by Roenick's performance that he refused to move it back and that night slept in the "room" beside the elevator.

•   •   •

Ken Wreggett's professional career got off to a rocky start. He and Alan Bester were the goaltenders for the Toronto Maple Leafs during some of their worst years – the era in which Gerry McNamara was general manager.

For those of you who are lucky enough not to remember McNamara, probably all you need to know is that he once went to court to prove he was brain-damaged.

Wreggett and Bester were kids who should have been brought along carefully, then eased into the NHL. Instead, they were shoved into front-line action. Neither fared well as a result.

The pair made their first NHL appearance in the 1983–84 season, and despite occasional banishments to the minors, they were the mainstays of the Leafs' goaltending corps for the next few years. Wreggett lasted with the Leafs until 1989, when he was traded to the Philadelphia Flyers. A year later, Bester was sent to the Detroit Red Wings.

But upon leaving the Leafs, their careers went in different directions. Bester played only fourteen more NHL games, whereas Wreggett blossomed and became a solid NHL goalie. His record with the Leafs had been an appalling 55–112–17, but over the next twelve years, he won 170 games, lost 136, and tied 36.

I ran into him a few times over his career, but one of the games I remember best was his seventh-game victory in the 1995 playoffs when he was playing for the Pittsburgh Penguins.

The Washington Capitals had opened a 3–1 series lead, but the Penguins came back to tie the series, and in the seventh game, Wreggett was brilliant, shutting out the Capitals. By that time, he had an inner resolve that had never seemed apparent during his Leafs days.

Under his sweater that night, he was wearing a T-shirt that read, "Game 7. If you lose this one, you might as well have lost them all."

• • •

One of the toughest guys ever to play in the NHL was Dave Semenko, who spent most of his NHL career in Edmonton making sure that no one took any liberties with Wayne Gretzky.

In order to do this, Semenko had to be ready to take on the league's most effective enforcers. It was a duty he always fulfilled, and he rarely, if ever, lost a fight.

And how many teeth did he lose in the process? Not a one.

But he did lose teeth.

After retiring from active hockey in 1988, Semenko became a scout, but with nothing to do during the 1994 lockout, he took up skiing and whiled away his time on the slopes.

Schussing down the hill one day, Semenko did a face plant and knocked out his two front teeth. In typical hockey fashion, he picked up the wayward incisors, shoved them in his pocket, trooped off into Banff, and had a dentist re-insert them.

It wasn't long before the patient, and his teeth, were back on the slopes.

•  •  •

Marty McSorley was another enforcer who protected Gretzky in Edmonton and subsequently in Los Angeles. In fact, it was Gretzky who insisted that McSorley be included in the famous "trade" – actually more of a sale – that sent him to the Kings in 1988.

Most of the deal to trade Gretzky had already been arranged, and Gretzky was in the office of Bruce McNall, the owner of the Kings, when the final aspects were being negotiated. McNall was on the speaker phone with Oilers owner Peter Pocklington, who didn't know that Gretzky was listening. At one point, Gretzky started waving his arms and McNall put Pocklington on hold. "Get him to put Marty in the deal," Gretzky said to McNall.

McNall made the request. Pocklington considered the possibility but said he'd have to discuss the matter with Oilers general manager Glen Sather.

Gretzky again signalled to McNall to put Pocklington on hold. "You can't let him do that," he said. "Glen would never agree to letting Marty go. You have to tell Peter that either Marty gets included or the deal is off."

McNall did as he was told and Pocklington acceded.

• • •

McSorley's presence was crucial to Gretzky's success in Los Angeles. I had players from other teams tell me that they felt a foot taller if they went into Los Angeles and McSorley was out of the lineup for some reason. That reason could have been an injury, but it was just as likely to have been a suspension.

He could be dangerous, and his NHL opponents knew that only too well. McSorley, no shrinking violet when it comes to discussing his contributions, is proud of his contribution to Gretzky's successes. "There's no way I'm taking credit for the things that Wayne did," he said. "He was a fantastic player and a tremendous talent. But I did make sure that he got a chance to use that talent.

"I like to think that if it hadn't been for me, he wouldn't have set all those records, not because I had anything to do with them directly, but because if it hadn't been for me, he wouldn't have been in the lineup as often and he wouldn't have been playing injury-free.

"At the first hint of somebody taking any liberty with him, I'd skate past the other team's bench and say, 'That's not happening tonight, guys. If anybody thinks it is, come on over right now and we'll discuss it.' That usually put an end to it."

Not many people wanted to get into a discussion with McSorley. His discussions tended to become physical in a hurry.

•  •  •

There are those who say fighting has no place in hockey, that people like McSorley should be banned from using their fists.

In a perfect world, that might be the case. But the NHL is far from perfect, and the inescapable fact is that hockey is a physical game. Body checks are allowed. Physical impediments are allowed within certain parameters. There's a large grey area between what is clearly legal and what is clearly illegal. Look at what happened to the other stars.

Mario Lemieux was banged around so much that he announced publicly that he was sick of it and called the NHL "a garage league."

Sidney Crosby suffered concussions. So did Eric Lindros.

In fact, many of the NHL's top scorers in recent years have been battered around to the point that they have been forced out of the game for extended stretches while they recover from injuries.

Gretzky, on the other hand, suffered only one serious injury, which came in the 1991 Canada Cup. He suffered a cracked vertebra when Team USA defenceman Gary Suter ran him into the boards from behind.

Two important points have to be made about that hit. First, Team Canada had no true enforcers playing for it. So Suter felt safe from retaliation. Second, the game was played under international rules, which essentially ban fighting.

• • •

McSorley, by the way, was responsible for one stage in the evolution of the existing rule requiring tie-down sweaters. Nowadays, if a player's sweater comes off during a fight, he is given a ten-minute misconduct in addition to whatever other penalties he might have earned.

It all started with McSorley making sweater modifications. "The most important thing to remember," he explained, "is that the real tough guys *want* to fight." (The NHL's heavyweights refer to themselves as "tough guys," not "enforcers" and certainly not "goons.")

"Guys who don't, want to grab. I don't want to go to the penalty box for five minutes because some guy tried to earn brownie points with his coach by throwing two punches, then hanging on.

"If a guy is hanging on," continued McSorley, "a tough guy will take a punch or two to get the fight going. That's why the tough guys hate linesmen who get in there early."

So McSorley, being a genuine tough guy, took to wearing a goalie sweater.

An opponent could try to hang on by grabbing his sleeves, but goalies wear sweaters with arms like a kimono to allow for all the padding they wear. Those sleeves were so baggy, McSorley could run through the entire semaphore alphabet while someone was holding on to them.

The other attribute of a goalie sweater is that it has a large neck opening and would therefore easily slip over that tiny Jofa helmet that McSorley wore. It was a helmet that was so useless as protection that it was banned by the league, but McSorley was allowed to continue wearing it under a grandfather clause.

Because the NHL always tries to crack down on someone who does well, the league decided to make baggy sweaters like McSorley's illegal.

Dave Brown, another elite tough guy, went the other way. He wore sweaters so tight that you could see looser clothes on the Playboy Channel – when you see them at all. Then he sprayed his sweater with silicon to make it slippery.

There was no way an opponent could tie him up by grabbing his sweater.

The Buffalo Sabres' enforcer at the time, Rob Ray, came up with his own solution. He simply took off his sweater.

At the initiation of hostilities, he would go into a crouch so that the first couple of blows bounced off his helmet. Then in a flurry of squirming reminiscent of Houdini shedding a strait jacket, the sweater and shoulder pads would both be gone, and Ray would be swinging freely, raining punches on a bewildered opponent left holding a pile of soggy laundry in his hands.

Eventually, however, the league killed all these tactics. Now guys fight fully clothed face to face, bounce a few punches off each other's helmets, and head for the box.

But the pacifists are happy because the game isn't glorifying fighting any more. Unfortunately, more often than not, the pacifists don't watch hockey.

• • •

In my book *I Am Not Making This Up*, I included a lot of anecdotes about Wayne Gretzky.

I occasionally had some misgivings about doing so. I thought that perhaps because I know him so well, my own admiration of him might be colouring my judgment. But the editors assured me that this was not the case, and then, when the book was published, so did the readers.

Not only was the feedback totally in favour, a number of people suggested that I should do a book completely devoted to Gretzky stories.

Although I would have no objection to such a project, I wouldn't want to do it without his direct involvement, and at the moment, he is focusing on being a father to his five children.

Nevertheless, you can rest assured that as this book goes on, there will be a number of Gretzky anecdotes.

And why not? A study done in early 2011 showed that even twelve years after his retirement, he is still the most identifiable hockey player in the world.

He is also the most marketable player. If you want someone to endorse your product, no one will get a better consumer response – not Alexander Ovechkin, not Sidney Crosby, not even Mario Lemieux.

When Gretzky turned fifty years old on January 26, 2011, it was almost a national holiday in Canada. Newspapers devoted large segments to retrospectives. The Canadian

Press distributed a video clip to its newspaper subscribers of Don Cherry singing "Happy Birthday" to Wayne Gretzky. The *Globe and Mail*'s website featured the video prominently.

Without exception, every news broadcast I heard that day – on television and radio, in English and in French – mentioned the Gretzky milestone. The TV sports networks aired specials on Gretzky's career, and the call-in radio shows discussed little else. For instance, here is the lineup of people who did full-segment interviews – about twenty minutes each – on the Fan 590 in Toronto on that day: former teammate Mark Messier; the Edmonton Oilers' play-by-play announcer during the Gretzky era, Rod Phillips; Gretzky's coach for much of his time with the Los Angeles Kings, Barry Melrose; another former teammate, Kevin Lowe; and, of course, his father, Walter Gretzky.

And that was just in the morning!

Gretzky discussions in various forms continued for the rest of the day.

So there will be a number of Gretzky stories in this book – and this time, I have no reservations about including them.

•   •   •

When a team advances to the Stanley Cup finals, it is standard procedure for the local paper to crank up its coverage. Editors order up pre-series supplements full of retrospectives, photo essays, and statistics. Once the series starts, busloads of reporters are sent to cover the game. Most of them are instructed to focus on a specific area: the losing coach, the guy who scored the game-winning goal, the crowd reaction, even the anthem singer. There's no limit to what a creative editor can dream up as the basis for a story at that time of year.

To do all this requires the hijacking of staffers from other departments within the paper, and as a result, especially in some of the American cities, much of the coverage is produced by people who have little or no familiarity with hockey.

After the game, many of them visit the hospitality suite – generally referred to as the hostility suite – that the league provides at a nearby hotel. It goes without saying that these post-game get-togethers – which are standard in all the major-league sports – are usually well attended. After all, they offer free drinks and free food. It's as close to heaven as a sportswriter is ever likely to come.

During the 1999 Stanley Cup final in Dallas, a number of media people were sitting at a large table when a local writer asked if he could take an empty seat. Hockey writers tend to be an amiable bunch – especially when they're being served free food and free beer – and not only was he encouraged to join us, every effort was made to include him in the conversation.

Before long, we learned that he was getting his first exposure to hockey. "What do you normally cover?" he was asked.

"Executions," he said.

Texas, it seems, usually has more than three hundred executions a year, and it was this guy's job to make sure the populace was kept abreast of the proceedings in as many cases as possible.

It brought to mind the old line of Lou Holtz, an American college-football coach. When asked after a game what he thought of his team's execution, he said, "I'm in favour of it."

# CHAPTER NINE

*The more self-evident a fact might appear to the layman,*
*the more vigorously must the conscientious lawyer contest it.*
John le Carré, *Single and Single*

**When the Phoenix Coyotes** were facing bankruptcy in May 2009, there was no doubt that they would
soon move to southern Ontario. At least that was the case
if you listened to almost anybody in southern Ontario.

Jim Balsillie, the CEO of Research In Motion, which you
might know better as the company that makes the ubiqui-
tous BlackBerry, had put in a bid of $212.5 million U.S. for
the Coyotes. A self-made billionaire, Balsillie clearly had the
financial wherewithal not only to purchase an NHL team but
also, from a business point of view, to run it properly.

The consensus in southern Ontario was rock solid. The
region is a well-populated hockey hotbed and would support
a second team just as strongly as it supports the Toronto
Maple Leafs. The leasing arrangements were in place to
allow the Coyotes to use the Copps Coliseum in Hamilton
as their home until a new arena could be built. Even the

"anchor corporate partners," Labatt Breweries and Home
Hardware, climbed aboard the Balsillie bandwagon.

What could possibly go wrong?

The National Hockey League's board of governors,
that's what.

At the time, I was part of a regular show on The Score
TV network, and I kept saying again and again that the
Coyotes would not be leaving Arizona. The others on
the show argued vehemently. It made too much sense not
to happen, they said.

A few small, good-natured bets were made (which
were never paid off, by the way).

Almost everyone I met disagreed with me as well. But
they, like the people at The Score, were fans. There's nothing
wrong with that, but when it comes to moving hockey
teams, fans don't make the decisions. The NHL's governors do. And they're not fans; they're investors.

•  •  •

As the Arizona court proceedings dragged on throughout
the summer, the opinion in southern Ontario never
changed. But the NHL battled Balsillie every step of the
way, and finally, thanks to a series of rulings in bankruptcy
court by Judge Redfield T. Baum, the NHL won.

Balsillie had been rejected. NHL commissioner Gary
Bettman, front and centre for the league throughout the
legal marathon, had come out on top.

Bettman didn't oppose Balsillie in order to allow his league to put a different owner in place. There was no serious prospective owner on the horizon. In fact, after the court decision, the league itself had to run the Coyotes for well over a year.

But there were two reasons that the NHL fought so hard against Balsillie. One had to do with this specific case. The other comes into play every time someone suggests that it might be a good idea to move a U.S.–based team to Canada.

In general, the first reason is that in some ways, the NHL is like the mafia. It's a closed society with a strict code of what the mafia calls *omertà* – silence. Balsillie talked a lot about what he intended to do – just as he did when he was in the running to purchase other NHL teams. There are stringent qualifications for NHL (and mafia) membership, and you have to show respect for the organization. Balsillie had the primary qualification – lots of money – but he didn't show respect.

The second reason is that the governors want an American league. If they had to endure six Canadian teams, so be it. But they hadn't the slightest intention of allowing another Canadian team to enter the league, until they were forced to do so when Bettman was unable to find even one person in the entire United States who would purchase the Atlanta Thrashers in 2011.

But when Balsillie was making his overtures, other prospective buyers appeared to be available.

Only one thing could make them change their mind on that point: money. Lots and lots of money. And even at $212.5 million, Jim Balsillie hadn't reached that point.

Had Balsillie been giving that money to the thirty NHL governors, it would have been interesting to see if this would have changed their collective minds. But it wouldn't have gone to them. It would have gone to the guy who was selling the Coyotes. No dice.

• • •

Jim Balsillie first came to the NHL's attention midway through the 2005–06 season when he started kicking tires on the Pittsburgh Penguins.

Those were dark days for the league, which was trying to recapture fan support after Bettman killed the 2004–05 season. At that time, the Penguins were the most dilapidated franchise in the NHL. They had a country-club reputation and a history of bankruptcies. They played in the oldest, least economical arena in the NHL.

Sidney Crosby was on the team but was a rookie and still unproven. Evgeni Malkin was still playing in Magnitogorsk. The potential of goaltender Marc-André Fleury was in doubt after he won only four of twenty-one games in his first NHL season.

Onto the scene strode Jim Balsillie, publicly announcing that he was willing to pay $175 million U.S. for the Penguins. The governors' eyes widened. Even Gary Bettman had to take notice. The financial world is based on precedents, and if the Penguins were worth $175 million, what would be the price for a real franchise?

It didn't take the league's number-crunchers long to figure it out. If the sale of the Penguins to Balsillie were to be approved by the board of governors, the NHL would suddenly be worth at least a whopping $3 billion more than it had been prior to the lockout.

And really, that was the low end, a very conservative evaluation.

The pre-lockout Penguins were valued at $75 million. Even at that price, no one wanted them. Now they were selling for $175 million.

In percentage terms, the Penguins' value rose 133 per cent. If that figure were extrapolated league-wide, the NHL franchises may be worth $7 or $8 billion more than they used to be.

But even on a flat arithmetical scale, a $100 million increase per franchise spread across thirty franchises is $3 billion.

So Bettman, to whom hockey is a series of economic opportunities encumbered by a bunch of athletes, wasn't about to pass up Balsillie's involvement in the league.

But the arrival of Balsillie was soon revealed to be something less than the godsend it had seemed to be.

What Balsillie really wanted was increased NHL involvement in Canada, and to further that end, he wanted to move the Penguins to southern Ontario.

Bettman was appalled by such a concept. For one thing, he was – and continues to be – dead set against increasing Canadian involvement. For another, he covets stability and doesn't like to see franchises move anywhere, even within the United States. So he suddenly found himself in duck mode – looking cool and unruffled on the surface but paddling furiously under water.

To the casual observer, he was calmly trying to make sure that anyone willing to listen was made aware of the economic resurgence of the NHL as illustrated by the sale of the Penguins. But out of sight, he was trying to make certain that the league would get Balsillie to buy the Penguins and then block any chance of moving them.

• • •

Balsillie and Penguins owner Mario Lemieux had already agreed on the sale terms when Bettman got involved. He asked Balsillie to support an existing bid by a company called Isle of Capri Entertainment, which had offered to build a new arena for the Penguins in return for slot-machine rights.

That didn't really present a problem. The bottom line on that deal was that it would make the Penguins profitable. Balsillie would have a new arena for his team. The catch was that the franchise would have to stay in Pittsburgh. They were the draw that would help bring people into Isle of Capri's casino. (Bettman's opposition to gambling apparently doesn't extend to prospective team purchasers.)

Bettman decided that he would negotiate the arena deal on Balsillie's behalf and that as part of the agreement to finalize the sale the league would have the right to take over the team if necessary.

To Bettman's mind, that takeover could be implemented if Balsillie decided to move the Penguins out of town.

On December 15, 2006, Balsillie withdrew his offer to buy the team.

After having visions of huge windfall profits waved before their eyes, the governors were angry when Balsillie walked away.

Strike one.

• • •

A little more than a year later, Balsillie was looking at another target, the Nashville Predators.

The Predators have always struggled financially, even though the franchise received an astonishingly lucrative package from the city of Nashville, having been given a combined arena and practice facility, a complex that was built at a cost to the taxpayers of approximately $160 million U.S.

On May 23, 2007, Balsillie announced that he had reached a tentative agreement with Predators owner Craig Leipold to buy the team.

Leipold had been one of the hard-liners during the lockout, holding firmly to the theory that the NHL players, like the city of Nashville, should make significant concessions in order to facilitate his personal financial well-being. Again, Balsillie made no secret of his intentions. Even though he didn't make a lot of public pronouncements himself, he had a lawyer who repeatedly fed "not-for-attribution" statements to the media and whose cell phone number was on every hockey columnist's speed dial.

Balsillie wanted to move the Predators to southern Ontario. This time, there was no pretence of hanging around for a while. If the deal went through, the Predators would open the 2007–08 season in Hamilton. Hamilton mayor Fred Eisenberger even made an announcement saying that this was Balsillie's intention.

Once again, the governors were livid. Once again, Balsillie had broken the code of *omertà*. The deal was far from being done, but he was already discussing it publicly. The governors had no doubt where all the Predators-to-Hamilton stories were coming from. To them, Balsillie was an anathema. Their idol was Los Angeles Kings owner Philip Anschutz. The adjective most often used to describe Anschutz is "reclusive."

Balsillie carried on, either oblivious or indifferent to the governors' reactions.

Less than a month after the first leak of the story, Balsillie was accepting deposits on season tickets to the Hamilton Predators. He started selling luxury boxes. The intention was to make it clear that the market in southern Ontario far exceeded the market in Nashville.

That was Balsillie's interpretation of his actions. The interpretation placed on the act by the governors was that Balsillie was trying to publicly embarrass them by showing the world that they had made a mistake when they put the team in Nashville.

There is little doubt that the NHL governors expressed that view rather forcefully to Leipold and pointed out that they had shut down the league for a year so that people like him could be in a better position to compete.

On June 22, Leipold pulled out of any deal with Balsillie. He released a statement, saying, "We did send the NHL a letter today requesting that it not do any further due diligence on Jim Balsillie's offer for the Nashville Predators until we reach a binding agreement. If Jim is interested in reaching a binding agreement, we are prepared to move forward."

Six days later, there was another announcement. Craig Leipold would not be reaching any binding agreements with Jim Balsillie.

Strike two.

•  •  •

Less than a week later, Leipold did sell the team. But the buyer wasn't Balsillie. Instead, it was a deal more to the governors' liking. It went to one of their kind, a financier, not one of those annoying high-tech guys. The purchaser was William DelBiaggio, known to one and all by his nickname of Boots.

Good old Boots was going to fork over $190 million of his extensive personal wealth for the Predators and operate them in the tried-and-true fashion that the governors so admire.

Within a year, Boots was busy filing for Chapter 11 bankruptcy protection.

Like a few other former NHL governors, he's now in jail serving time for fraud. In his case, the sentence was a little more than eight years – ninety-seven months to be precise.

•   •   •

After all this, it came as no surprise to anyone familiar with the inner workings of the National Hockey League that Balsillie would not be welcomed with open arms when he produced a bid for the Coyotes.

By prowling around the league, showing up like a shark smelling blood wherever franchises were in trouble, he had focused public attention on the NHL's mistakes.

Worse still, he had either directly or indirectly made his intentions public. He had already made it clear that if he were to be allowed into their exclusive community, he could not be counted on to follow their rules obediently.

The governors may know nothing about hockey, but they do know about business and they know about money.

They know that Al Davis cost the National Football League owners billions of dollars by being a rebel owner. They'd rather dig into their pockets to support a troubled franchise than sell that franchise to a rebel owner.

They know also that Balsillie, like Davis, is not afraid to use the courts to follow a course of action that he feels is just, even if, to the more conservative elements of society, that cause seems unreasonable.

As businessmen, they would know that, in his capacity as CEO of Research In Motion, Balsillie once refused to accept a court-ordered settlement of $23 million U.S. for patent infringement.

Despite the advice of many around him to pay up and go on his way, he fought the decision all the way to the U.S. Supreme Court – and lost all the way.

Research In Motion finally paid a settlement of $612.5 million, not counting the legal fees.

Many fans assume that when Gary Bettman was front and centre in the fight against Jim Balsillie in Phoenix, he was doing it out of personal dislike.

Certainly, it has been widely reported that Bettman has a personal dislike for Balsillie. But that's not why he was acting as he did. He was doing it because the thirty governors for whom he works wanted him to do so.

After Pittsburgh and Nashville, they wanted no part of Jim Balsillie.

Strike three.

# CHAPTER TEN

*It beats all how some folks think that making or getting*
*money is a kind of game where there are not any rules at all.*
William Faulkner, *Light in August*

**In Gary Bettman's view,** the best way to have a successful league is to have owners with deep pockets.

Considering the speed with which the player salaries keep rising, no matter what kind of collective bargaining agreement Bettman negotiates, that's probably not a bad strategy. The problem with it is that the league ends up with owners who know nothing about hockey. In fact, some of them brag that until they entered into the process of buying a team, they had never seen a game.

Does this matter? It does if you have an owner who decides that he'll get involved with the running of the team. And more often than not, that's exactly what happens.

The kind of people who have amassed billions of dollars – or at least hundreds of millions – are not used to taking orders from anyone else. They have done well in their chosen business – be it movie rentals or computer

software or securities fraud – and therefore see no reason
to accept advice about hockey from someone whose only
qualification is that he has spent his life in the game.
What would he know?

The last time the New York Islanders were sold, they
went to a pair of entrepreneurs, Charles Wang and Sanjay
Kumar.

Kumar is no longer with the team. He's busy serving
a twelve-year term for a $2.2 billion fraud.

Twelve years seems a bit excessive. After all, who among
us doesn't misplace a billion or two now and then? And
those thirty-five-day months that were used in the account-
ing procedures were no doubt just a well-intentioned
attempt to round out the calendar. Why bother with months
of anywhere from twenty-eight to thirty-one days when a
nice five-week month is so much more convenient?

In addition to the prison sentence, Kumar was fined
$8 million and ordered to pay $798.6 million in restitu-
tion. He sold his fifty-eight-foot yacht, two Ferraris, and
investment accounts to pay the first $50 million.

In Canada, he'd probably have to serve a month or so
if it weren't too inconvenient for him. In the United
States, he'll have to serve more than ten years plus two
months, and even though he appealed (who doesn't?), the
appeal failed.

He's just the latest example of a point I've often made.
In the other sports, players go to jail. In hockey, it's the
owners who go to jail.

• • •

As is usually the case in such matters, the partners in the Islanders' affair didn't exactly throw their unconditional support behind each other. Kumar blamed Wang. Wang blamed Kumar.

But Kumar was the one who went to jail. Wang didn't. He stayed out to help run the Islanders. The pair purchased the Islanders in 2000, and thanks to Wang's guidance, the team is already in a position to win a playoff round some day. It would be the first playoff win under Wang's stewardship, assuming they do it while he's still in control.

But it should not be assumed that this long-term incompetence came about through lack of vision. It was, after all, his idea to have his scouts go to Japan to see if they could get a sumo wrestler to come and stand in goal for the Islanders. Apparently no one had explained to him that if you're a freak of nature, you play basketball, not hockey. When he failed to get a sumo wrestler, Wang gave Rick DiPietro a fifteen-year, $67.5 million contract to be the Islanders' goalie.

DiPietro has been a much-injured disappointment. He has averaged twenty-eight games a season, and his record is in the .500 range. Granted, there was no way Wang could have foreseen DiPietro's injuries, but on the other hand, that's why hockey people don't give out fifteen-year contracts.

Wang was also concerned by the fact that hockey has its violent moments. Apparently, his sporting knowledge hadn't extended to the realization that there are fights in hockey.

Accordingly, he got involved with the league's decision-making process and tried to impose a rule that would require every NHL player who got into a fight to take an anger-management course.

Honestly. He did that.

And you wonder why the Islanders are so bad?

•  •  •

When the Olympic Games were held in Seoul in 1988, the CBC sent its usual horde of broadcasters. This was the era before Nancy Lee was brought in as head of CBC Sports, so at that time, the network had a lot of sports properties, and the right to broadcast the Olympics was one of them.

As is usually the case at the Olympics, the meals in the media village are respectable enough, but when you're in a foreign country, you want to try out the local food. So, a couple of CBC guys picked a nearby restaurant at random and, despite the language problem, managed to let it be known that they wanted some lunch.

The waiter spoke only the most basic English, and they spoke no Korean, but by the use of sign language and some pointing at the menu, they managed to agree that they would have a form of Korean pasta.

It arrived piping hot and looked appetizing, but one of the guys had some concerns and called the waiter over. The language problem still existed, but he did manage to get his point across. Essentially, what he said was: "I'm Jewish and this looks like pork to me. Can you ask the chef to make sure it's not pork?"

The waiter smiled and hustled off. Not wanting his meal to get cold, the other guy dug in and was well into it by the time the waiter returned.

He was beaming. "Not pork," he said with a great deal of satisfaction. "Dog."

The story spread through the media centre like wildfire, and, media people being what they are, they had no shortage of observations.

"In Korea," said one, "when you order a hot dog, you get a hot dog."

Or the variation, "In Korea, when you ask for chow, you get a chow."

There were also a number of suggestions about other items that might be found on the menu in Korean restaurants:

Collie-flower
German shepherd pie
Lox and beagles
Singapore poodles
Cocker-au-vin
Springer rolls

Grated Dane

Whippet cream

Broc-collie

Boston cream terrier

And for breakfast, of course, Special K-9

•   •   •

It's an idea so simple, even Gary Bettman approves of it.

In fact, Bettman once tried to get the National Hockey League's board of governors to approve it, but those eminent gentlemen, hockey sages all, wouldn't go for it.

The concept is this: Make every game worth three points. Simple, isn't it?

But under today's rules, if a game is won in regulation time, the winner gets two points; the loser gets none. Some nights the game is won in overtime, or in a shootout. In that case, the winner gets two points. The loser gets one.

Why not shift to the more logical, the more equitable, and the more reasonable system of handing out three points in every game?

In effect, the league would be saying to its players before every game, "Okay, guys. We're handing out three points tonight. How you divide them is up to you. If you're good enough to win in regulation time, you get all three. If you need to go past that, you'll get two if you win, and one if you lose."

It would certainly help maintain fan interest throughout the season. Ever since the current system was put in place, a team that slipped ten points out of a playoff spot has had almost no chance of advancing to the post-season.

In fact, the puckheads who spend their time juggling sports numbers have worked out that the chance of a team overcoming a ten-point deficit is approximately 6 per cent. Therefore, even if it's only December and your favourite team is ten points out, you can pretty well rule out any hope of watching them compete in the playoffs.

Even if they win a few games and start to move up a bit, they get only two points per win. Teams ahead of them in the standings will be playing each other, and on many nights, even the losing team will get a point, while the winning team gets two.

It's like running up a down escalator. You'll make up some ground, but it's an awfully slow process; and in the case of hockey, with its eighty-two-game season, you'll run out of time before you run out of steps.

But look at what would happen if you were getting three points for a win. You'd be making up points every time you came through with a regulation-time victory. You'd be picking up a point on a team that won in a shootout and two points on its *losing* opponent. Now you're running up an *up* escalator.

It would provide a better spectacle for the fans as well. There is no suggestion here that today's NHL games aren't intense and hard-fought. But they'd become even more so if a team knew that cruising into overtime with a guaranteed point wasn't such an attractive proposition.

We've all seen games that are tied in the late stages and neither team is willing to pull out the stops. Instead, they sit back, play safe, and adopt a grab-a-point approach. But if three points were on the line, a team that needed to climb in the standings would mount a furious attack in those late stages of a tie game, instead of sitting back and playing not to lose.

Why did the governors not accept Bettman's proposal? Well, for one thing, it was part of the package that introduced shootouts in 2000, and the owners felt that they were already making radical changes. They didn't want to be too revolutionary all at once.

The other was that they had been convinced that a three-point win would somehow upset the purists because it would "distort" the record book.

Indeed, it would. But the governors had already upset the purists when they introduced the shootout. Furthermore, the record book had often been distorted over the years as the length of the season changed from fifty games to seventy-two to eighty to eighty-two. But the old records weren't invalidated. They were simply kept differently and had different reference points.

And really, there's nothing wrong with that. We live in a changing world, and sports have to evolve, just like everything else. The game doesn't have a rover any more either. And helmets are mandatory. Sometimes, you have to move on.

Oddly enough, there are also people who say they don't like the three-point concept because it rewards failure. These people say that they are purists and they don't like the idea of a point being awarded to the loser if the game goes past sixty minutes.

But they've been making the same complaints since 2000, and if they're such purists, they should know that hockey has always awarded a point for a tie after sixty minutes. That point is not a reward for losing; it's a reward for playing the full sixty minutes and not being outscored. That's the way hockey has always been.

In Europe, the various soccer associations fought the play-not-to-lose mindset by awarding three points for a victory, and it changed the nature of the game. Instead of the plodding games where players pull back at the first opportunity and take a defence-first attitude, teams now go for the three points. They have to because the approach has changed. In soccer's old days, if you tied every game, you'd be back next year. If you tie every game now, you'll probably be relegated.

In hockey, you don't get relegated. But the three-point concept would keep more teams in the playoff hunt, increase the intensity of the games, and provide a much more logical approach. Its time has come.

• • •

When you get right down to it, revamping the NHL record book by incorporating the changes the game has undergone over the decades might not be a bad idea. For instance, in the last couple of seasons, no rookie has broken onto the scene the way Sidney Crosby and Alexander Ovechkin did in 2005–06 when each cracked the 100-point barrier.

But the way young players continue to exhibit marvellous skills, it won't be long before another Ovechkin or Crosby lights up the league as a rookie. When that happens, as was the case when Ovechkin came in, there will be talk about how difficult it is to break Teemu Selanne's rookie record of 132 points.

As far as the nature of the quest is concerned, that statement is accurate. But when it comes to the number, it's accurate from a technical point of view only.

The NHL of an earlier era was run no more sensibly than the NHL of this era. After the 1979 merger with the World Hockey Association (which was really a takeover but was called a merger to keep anti-trust lawyers happy), the NHL decreed that no WHA player could be considered a rookie.

As a result, when Wayne Gretzky started the 1979–80 NHL season as an eighteen-year-old, he was ineligible for rookie awards. Gretzky scored 51 goals and added 86 assists that season for 137 points.

Most hockey people believe he even won the scoring title. He had the same number of points as Marcel Dionne, but Dionne had more goals and was therefore given the award. No one questions Dionne's goal total, but there is a lot of doubt about his assist total. In Los Angeles in those days, the franchise was desperate for support and there have been suggestions that Dionne's assist total was inflated. Still, no one knows with certainty so perhaps it's just a hockey version of an urban myth.

What is indisputable is that if the NHL were honest, Gretzky's 137 points would be the rookie record, not Selanne's 132.

Today's NHL governors could overturn that earlier ruling if they wanted to do so. After all, it's just a matter of a change in the record book – a change that would compensate for the lack of common sense among their predecessors.

It was a monumentally stupid decision to make an eighteen-year-old ineligible for rookie awards in the first place. After all, he couldn't have played in the NHL any sooner. The league had – and still has – a rule prohibiting participation by players under eighteen.

But the NHL has always taken a cavalier approach to its record book. That's why there are never any asterisks, even though the circumstances under which the records were set are constantly changing.

Selanne, by the way, came to the NHL after fulfilling his military commitments in Finland. In his record-setting season, he was twenty-two.

•   •   •

There are many reasons why Scott Bowman has been such a successful coach over the years.

There are those who disparage him and say that he had such great players on his team that he could hardly help but win. That conveniently ignores the fact that when Guy Lafleur broke into the NHL, he didn't come close to living up to his billing. In fact, he wasn't much above the ordinary. It was under Bowman's tutelage that he blossomed into a superstar.

It also ignores the fact that it was Scott Bowman who turned Steve Yzerman into one of the best team leaders in the history of hockey. Yzerman had suffered serious knee problems and had gone from being a great offensive player to a guy who appeared to be on his way out of hockey.

In his best year, 1988–89, Yzerman had racked up 155 points. But by the 1994–95 season, he was down to 38 points in forty-seven games. He had lost a step, and much of his brilliance had faded.

It was Bowman who turned Yzerman into a solid two-way player, almost certainly the most complete two-way player in the game. Yzerman captained the Red Wings to their first Stanley Cup in forty-two years and then two more after that before he joined the Wings' front office in 2006. Yzerman also played a major role in Canada's 2004 Olympic gold medal, the country's first in fifty years. He had a great series, even though his knee was so bad by that point that he could hardly walk.

As he hobbled along the day before the gold-medal game, I asked him, "Are you going to be able to play tomorrow, Stevie?" He looked at me as if that was the dumbest question he had ever heard. In retrospect, it probably was.

•   •   •

Bowman's primary tactic was this: He decided which player on his team had the most talent, then he let him do whatever he wanted to do.

Guy Lafleur wanted to come to the rink early and sit around all afternoon smoking heavily. Bowman didn't argue.

Most of the time, Mario Lemieux didn't want to practise. As a result, when Bowman was the coach in Pittsburgh, Lemieux rarely practised. He went on the ice occasionally, but he determined his own practice schedule.

Yzerman simply wanted to continue his career despite considerable outside pressure to hang up his skates. Bowman told Yzerman that he was welcome to stick around. But in every case, he also told the player, "I expect you to be the best."

In essence, Bowman said to these guys, "You've got no excuses. You come and go when you want. You choose your roommate or live alone, I don't care. Decide when and if you'll practise. Prepare for games in whatever manner you think best. After all that, if you're not the best, what's your excuse?"

If you look back at Stanley Cup winners over the years, you don't often find a team that was successful when its superstar didn't play well. And when you look back at Bowman's Stanley Cup winners, you always find his resident superstar leading the way.

•  •  •

There is a bar in Toronto – which I'd better not identify – where a lot of hockey writers tend to go after Leafs games. It has two very large televisions and a compliant owner who lets us decide on the programming. It serves decent food into the wee hours and has a good selection of beers.

One night in 2009, the place had a respectable late-night crowd. There were a few stragglers at the bar and in the seating area two sizeable groups. One of those groups consisted of hockey writers. The other looked as if it might contain a number of people who had just finished playing hockey. They were young and fit, were knocking back their beers at a steady rate, and had a few women for company. The two groups were at opposite ends of the large room.

We hadn't been there very long when tension mounted in the young-and-fit group. A couple of guys moved away from the table into an open area near the door and started arguing. The argument got louder, then became physical.

At that point, the benches cleared, so to speak. Everyone else in the group got up from the table and joined in.

Within seconds, it looked like a scene from one of those old western movies. People were grappling and rolling around on the floor. Others were jumping on top of the pile. One woman had a guy in a headlock and was forcing his head onto the floor while somebody else repeatedly delivered kidney punches. Threats and curses were flying, and every time the action appeared to be ready to die down, it flared up again.

Being hockey writers, we had only two available courses of action: (a) run away or (b) enjoy the spectacle.

Since the implementation of (a) would have meant leaving our drinks behind, we opted for (b), but after the brawl had been allowed to carry on for an acceptable amount of time, someone – probably someone from the *Toronto Star*, where knee-jerk pacifism is seen as a laudable concept – sidled over to the waitress, who was also standing there watching the proceedings. "Maybe we should call the cops," he said.

Her response was quick: "These are the cops."

• • •

Hockey fans love to debate – some might say argue – which was the best team in hockey history. Was it one of the New York Islanders' incarnations during the franchise's run of four consecutive Stanley Cups beginning in 1980?

Was it one of those high-flying Edmonton Oilers teams that followed on the heels of the Islanders dynasty?

Would it be a more recent team – the Detroit Red Wings or New Jersey Devils, for instance? What about that Montreal Canadiens team that won five consecutive Cups from 1956 to 1960?

If you ask hockey people, you're likely to get a lot of different answers. But the one team that seems to get mentioned more than any other is the 1976–77 Montreal Canadiens.

First, let's establish the criteria. We're looking for a team that had a greater degree of dominance than any others of that season. You can't directly compare a great player of one era to a great player of another era. It just doesn't work. Someone like Charlie Conacher, for instance, was a magnificent player in his day. But let's face it, Conacher, like everyone else on his 1932 Stanley Cup–winning Toronto Maple Leafs team (there are a few words that are rarely used in close conjunction these days), couldn't even make an NHL lineup today.

The game is much too fast, the shots are much too hard, the ability to skate backwards is much too important. Today's goalies wouldn't have the slightest problem stopping the floating wrist shots that were the staple of many of the game's early big scorers.

That doesn't diminish the skills possessed by the players of that earlier era. It just means that the game has changed so much over the years that those players didn't need to develop the skills that make today's top players so successful.

Similarly, you can't compare a team from 1950 to a team of today. The worst of the modern teams would have no trouble with those old teams. They'd skate circles around them; they'd push them off the puck all night long; they'd terrify the maskless goalies.

The modern players might lose the fights and suffer a few more slashes than they're used to, but today's refereeing would make the 1950 team pay dearly for its transgressions. The modern power play, with its rapid-fire puck movement, goalie screening, and rocket shots from the point would transform a bad situation into a downright embarrassment for the 1950 team.

What we have to do, therefore, is compare the teams within their own eras. When the Detroit Red Wings swept the Washington Capitals to win the Stanley Cup in 1998, for instance, were they that much better than the rest of the league? Probably not.

Using the criteria of the margin of superiority, the team that gets the most votes as the best team in hockey history – the one that left the rest of the league in its wake by the largest margin – was the 1976–77 Montreal Canadiens. The Canadiens' record that year was sixty wins, eight losses, and twelve ties. Considering the offensive talent that existed on that team, its record under today's rules probably would have been 72–8. It's hard to imagine them losing a shootout or in overtime.

Nine of that team's players were subsequently inducted into the Hockey Hall of Fame. The coach was Scott

Bowman, who is also in the Hall of Fame. The general manager was another legend – Sam Pollock. He's in there too. In goal for the 1976–77 Canadiens was Hall of Famer Ken Dryden. The defence was led by Serge Savard, Guy Lapointe, and Larry Robinson, all of whom are also in the Hall of Fame. Robinson was twice awarded the Norris Trophy as the NHL's best defenceman.

The offence was led by Guy Lafleur, three-time winner of the Art Ross Trophy and two-time winner of the Hart Trophy. He also twice won the Lester B. Pearson Trophy, which is awarded to the best player in the league in the view of the other players. In that memorable 1976–77 season, Lafleur won all three of those trophies in recognition of his outstanding production of 56 goals and 80 assists for 136 points. On his left wing was Steve Shutt, who had 60 goals that year. There was no Rocket Richard trophy for the league's top goal scorer in those days, but if there had been, Shutt would have won it. He also added 45 assists to the cause.

At centre was the incomparable Jacques Lemaire, the steady conscience of the line, always making sure that the offensive forays didn't leave the Canadiens defensively vulnerable while at the same time firing laser passes to Lafleur and Shutt. Even so, he was still an offensive force in his own right, scoring 34 goals and adding 41 assists.

That entire line is in the Hall of Fame, as are two other forwards off that team – Bob Gainey and Yvan Cournoyer. Gainey did not win the Frank J. Selke Trophy, awarded to the league's best defensive forward, with that 1977 team for the simple reason that it was not instituted until the following season. But since Gainey won the first Selke Trophy and the next three as well, it seems safe to say that he would also have won it in 1977 had it been available. By that stage of his career, Cournoyer was a specialty player whose blazing speed and offensive skills were not what they once had been. Yet, he was still such a considerable threat that any opposing team ignored him at its peril.

Even the next level of players was outstanding. Hockey fans who remember that era will agree that people like Doug Risebrough, Jimmy Roberts, Doug Jarvis, Pierre Mondou, Rejean Houle, Brian Engblom, and Bill Nyrop would have excelled on any team in the league.

In that entire 1976–77 season, the Canadiens lost only one home game. Because it came early in the season, no one paid much attention. It was just another Saturday night loss to the Boston Bruins. Such a development, while a matter of some concern in Montreal, was not a calamity.

The Bruins, coached by Don Cherry at the time, were about the only team the Canadiens had trouble with that year. Of their eight losses, three were inflicted by the Bruins. But when the playoffs rolled around, the Canadiens shrugged off the regular season results. They met the Bruins in the Stanley Cup final and swept them by an aggregate score of 16–6.

Of all the great teams in the history of the National Hockey League, none has been better than the 1976–77 Montreal Canadiens.

• • •

Over the years, Wayne Gretzky and I discussed many subjects, on and off the record. In some of his off-the-record
comments, he was occasionally critical of someone in
hockey. But I never, either on or off the record, heard him
criticize his coach.

As far as Gretzky was concerned, in order to be successful, a hockey team has to have someone in charge.
That someone has to be the coach, and by being critical of
the coach, especially if you're Wayne Gretzky, all you do is
undermine the stability of your own organization.

When Gretzky was in Edmonton, Glen Sather, like any
coach, would deliver a dressing-room tirade when he felt
that his club needed it. On those occasions, he would often
heap abuse on Gretzky. "That was all right," said Gretzky.
"Glen always knew the difference between the carrot and
the stick. He always knew which guys would play worse if
they were criticized and which guys would play better."

Sather also knew that it did no good to bully the lesser
lights. If the team wasn't going well, it wouldn't be the third
and fourth line that would turn the tide. Furthermore, if
he stayed away from the stars when he was dressing down
the team, it might foster resentment. So Sather consistently
went after Gretzky and Mark Messier. Jari Kurri got his
share of criticism as well.

When the Oilers won their first Stanley Cup, a carrot
was part of the design pattern on the ring. No stick. But

the stick had often been there. Barry Melrose, who coached Gretzky in Los Angeles, never had any problems with Gretzky either. "Of all the superstars," said Melrose, "I had the best guy. He just wanted to play. He didn't want to coach the team. He didn't want to be an owner. He didn't want to be a manager. He just wanted to be a player. Wayne never disrupted the team, even though he often had other commitments. He had to go and shoot commercials and do things like that, but he never once missed a practice."

•  •  •

I only ever heard of one instance in which Gretzky didn't accept his coach's criticism. And he wasn't the one who told me about it. In fact, he still doesn't talk about it.

It happened in Winnipeg on a night when the Los Angeles Kings were playing the Jets. Gretzky coughed up the puck and the Jets pounced on his mistake, broke in on Kings goaltender Kelly Hrudey, and scored. Gretzky was chasing the play, and when he got to the net, furious at himself, he broke his stick over the crossbar. Coach Robbie Ftorek benched him for the rest of the period.

In the dressing room between periods, Ftorek explained his action in front of the team. He said that a display of petulance like breaking a stick over the crossbar showed a loss of control. Players had to keep their emotions under control at all times, he said, and since Gretzky had been unable to do so, he had been punished by being benched for the remainder of the period.

"I'm not just a coach," said Ftorek in his usual condescending manner, "I'm a teacher."

"If you want to teach," snapped Gretzky, "go to the minors. I want to win."

•   •   •

It would seem that Ftorek later forgot his own lesson about maintaining composure under trying circumstances.

On January 29, 2000, by which time he was coaching the New Jersey Devils, Ftorek was incensed by a refereeing decision. One of his players, Jay Pandolfo, had been injured, and although he was lying on the ice, officials allowed play to continue. With the Devils at a disadvantage, the Detroit Red Wings scored.

Ftorek was so furious that after the usual amount of screaming at the referee he picked up the players' bench and threw it on the ice. Colin Campbell, the man in charge of NHL discipline at the time, fined Ftorek $10,000 and suspended him for a game. Campbell did not feel it necessary to announce that it was his job to be a teacher.

# CHAPTER ELEVEN

*Luxury is dangerous to people who have never known it and to whom its temptations are held out too suddenly.*
  W. Somerset Maugham, *Ashenden: The British Agent*

**I'd better not tell you** the name of this player, but if you know your hockey, you can probably work it out.

When Neil Smith was general manager of the New York Rangers, the team always stayed at the same hotel in Montreal. For his loyalty, Smith was duly rewarded with the penthouse suite, the best accommodation the hotel had to offer. But when the Rangers made their first trip to Montreal after acquiring the player in question, Smith went to the desk to pick up his key and was distressed to find that while he had a large, elegant suite, it was not the penthouse. He crowded into the elevator with a few of the New York players and glumly punched the button for his floor. The player in question leaned over and punched the penthouse button.

"What the hell?" fumed Smith. "I'm the general manager of this team. I'm the one who confirms the travel arrangements and brings the team to this hotel. How come I don't get the penthouse suite and you do?"

The player shrugged and quietly said, "I guess it's because I own the hotel."

•  •  •

One morning after a loss, Detroit Red Wings coach Scott Bowman told his team to leave the pucks where they were. They were going to do some skating. He divided the team into four groups, each of which contained one of the previous night's forward lines and a defenceman or two.

The fourth line was sent off to do a circuit of the rink. After forty seconds, Bowman blew his whistle. Next came the turn of the third-line group. They did about forty seconds as well. Then Bowman sent off the second line. They had to do about fifty seconds at full speed around the rink before Bowman stopped them.

Now it was time for the first line. For a full two minutes, Bowman kept them skating. Then the whole four-step process was repeated. And again. And again.

Finally, Bowman called the team together. The first-liners and the top defence pair were gasping. "Tired?" asked Bowman, glaring at them. "You didn't mind taking two-minute shifts last night."

End of message.

•  •  •

When I started covering hockey, the post-game drink for most players was beer. You'd go into the dressing room and in the middle of the room would be a trestle table with a couple of large tubs of beer on ice. More often than not, when you were talking to a player, he'd be taking swigs of beer while you were asking questions.

It was, of course, purely coincidental that if the team was in a hurry to get away for some reason, the media hung around the room longer than usual.

But beer acquisition was seen as part of the job description in those days. The writers who didn't have time to hang around the dressing room were duly appreciative of the cold beers we took back up to the press box.

It all changed in the early eighties when do-gooders masquerading as sportswriters started denouncing the link between hockey and alcohol. You know the stuff. The NHL encourages beer drinking. Hockey breeds alcoholics. And so on.

There is no beer in the dressing rooms now. But you might find some in the fridge in the general manager's office.

•   •   •

Even if the players didn't knock back a cold one in the dressing room, they often did so once they had left the building.

I was travelling with the Edmonton Oilers during their glory days of the eighties, and we were about to make the post-game bus trip from Long Island to Manhattan. "Where's the beer?" shouted someone as the bus began to fill up. There was no beer. "Gretz, we've got no beer," someone shouted.

"Well, I can't carry it by myself," said Gretzky as he wandered down the aisle towards the door.

The Long Island Marriott Hotel is adjacent to the Nassau County Coliseum, so Gretzky went into the hotel with a couple of other Oilers. They went to the bar, and Gretzky bought three cases of cold beer – at the usual exorbitant bar prices that hotels charge. The beer was brought back to the bus and distributed, but now another problem had arisen. Someone had parked illegally in the U-shaped driveway in front of the hotel and the bus couldn't get past. Again, a few volunteers were required. Four or five of the Oilers went outside, lifted the car off the driveway and onto the grass, then got back onto the bus.

Finally, we were on our way into Manhattan – everyone happily enjoying a couple of beers during the trip.

•  •  •

When you're a columnist for a major newspaper, you're generally allowed to write what you want. The columns get edited, as does everything else that goes into the paper, but changes are usually minor. If they're not, the columnist is invariably consulted on the matter.

But once in a while, for one reason or another, a

column gets spiked. The term goes back to the old days of newspapers when everything was typed onto a sheet of paper and unwanted sheets were put on a spike placed on the editing desk for that purpose.

In today's newspapers, columns aren't literally spiked, but the result is the same. The editor decides for some reason that he doesn't want it to run. It could be because the column isn't any good (rare). It could be because, through a lack of communication, someone else at the paper has written a similar column on the same subject (occasional). It could be because the editor is a complete idiot (almost always).

What follows here is a column I wrote at the *Toronto Sun* around the time of the 2005 NHL lockout. It required a bit of hockey knowledge to understand, and it took a bit of work to figure out what it was all about, which was apparently beyond the intellectual capabilities of the sports editor. Perhaps he didn't know that before Gary Bettman became commissioner of the NHL, he used to work for commissioner David Stern at the National Basketball Association head office.

Then again, perhaps he was right to spike the column. Judge for yourself.

David: Gary. Nice to see you. How's it going?
Gary:   It's a work in progress, David. How are you?
David: I'm glad you asked. Not bad, but I'm a bit worried.
Gary:   Worried? Worried about what?

David: Well, about our league's popularity. As you know,
        not long ago we had such a small following, we
        had to pay to get our finals on network TV.
        Since then, we've soared, but now I'm worried
        about hockey.

Gary:  Hockey? I don't know a thing about hockey.
        I hardly know a puck from a beach ball. The
        NHL is a worry?

David: Yes. They're really gaining ground on us. They're
        almost as popular as us, and even though the
        New York Rangers haven't won the Stanley Cup
        in almost fifty years, this is 1993 and that run
        can't last. They might do it soon and then we
        could be in deep trouble.

Gary:  But, David, we got those union dimwits to agree
        to my salary-cap concept and our game is
        popular.

David: It is at the moment, Gary, but that's why I'm
        the NBA president and you're a vice-president.
        I have some vision and an ability to see the larger
        picture, which I don't think anyone has ever
        suggested is the case with you.

Gary:  So you think hockey might pass us in popularity?

David: I don't just think it, Gary, I'm sure of it. If
        hockey is left to its own devices, that is.

Gary:  But hockey is in a shambles. They just forced
        out John Ziegler as president. I'm not sure what
        you mean.

David: Well, it's this way. As you say, hockey is looking for someone to run the show. If we let events unfold in their natural course, there's no telling who they might get to run the league. They might break with a long-established precedent and get someone competent.

Gary: Hockey? Never.

David: Well, let's be sure. I want you to apply for the job.

Gary: Me?

David: Yes. You'd be perfect.

Gary: But I'm loyal to our league.

David: Exactly. And we wouldn't want that to ever change.

Gary: But how could I still be loyal if I were running hockey?

Davis: Have you ever read any spy stories, Gary?

Gary: No. But I've read a lot of torts.

David: How about the Trojan horse? Do you know that one?

Gary: Wait a minute. You mean you want me to get the job of running hockey and destroy the league from within?

David: There you go.

Gary: But I'm a senior vice-president here. I'm number three in the hierarchy. Hockey people aren't going to give their top job to a guy who's that high in a rival league.

David:  Gary, think about it. These are hockey people.
        Have you ever known them to do anything
        intelligent?

Gary:   Hmmm. OK. But what would I do if I got
        the job?

David:  I'd leave that up to you. Well, most of it anyway.
        But you could start by alienating the fans as
        much as possible. Lock out the officials, for
        example. Lock out the players.

Gary:   That might work.

David:  Sure, then you fiddle with the rules to make sure
        the skilled players can't show those skills. That
        way, the game becomes boring and no one will
        want to watch it. Hire another lawyer to handle
        discipline and tell him to be so lax that the fans
        get turned off when anything short of an axe-
        murder gets only a two-game suspension. That
        serves a double purpose. It makes sure the star
        players are injured a lot.

Gary:   And how about expanding into markets where
        no one likes the game? That would ruin the
        national TV ratings.

David:  Now you're getting it.

Gary:   And I could make sure the arenas play awful
        music at an ear-splitting level and I could get
        nets put up in the ends to block the views and
        I could . . .

David:  That's it, Gary. You've got the idea.

Gary:   But what happens if I'm so successful that I
        destroy the league? They'll fire me.
David:  Well, that will probably take you about fifteen
        years or so, but don't worry. There'll always be a
        job here for someone as loyal as you.

• • •

Hollywood has had its share of famous dogs over the
years – Lassie, Rin Tin Tin, and a host of others. But in
the hockey world, the most famous dog in history is Blue.
The original Blue.

She became famous when her owner, Don Cherry, was
the coach of the Boston Bruins. She has stayed famous
partly because her former owner makes sure of it and partly
because she appears in the opening segment of "Coach's
Corner" on *Hockey Night in Canada*. Furthermore, Don
talks about her at length in his book, *Don Cherry's Hockey
Stories and Stuff*.

Don has had a series of dogs named Blue since that
one, and he has loved them all, even though he has shifted
away from bull terriers in his most recent dogs.

Bull terriers are an astonishingly stupid dog, margin-
ally smarter than a pet rock, but they're loyal and tough,
so Don always liked them. For reasons that are hard to
understand if you own something like a border collie, bull
terriers always seem to engender a reciprocal sense of
loyalty in their owners. *Globe and Mail* columnist Christie

Blatchford has a bull terrier as well, and she's a total slave to his every whim.

The original Blue died in 1987 during the playoffs (totally inconsiderate of her), but Don kept it quiet for a few months before letting the cat out of the bag, so to speak. His reasoning, he explained, was that, "I didn't want to go through airports and places like that with everybody coming up and telling me how badly they felt about Blue. I felt bad enough as it was."

• • •

Blue's notoriety came about by accident. On a whim, Cherry took her to the Boston Gardens one day for the morning skate. "At first, they teased her a bit," recalled Cherry. "Then Wayne Cashman poked her with his stick and she bit the stick in two. That was the last time they ever teased her. From then on, she got cookies and stuff whenever she showed up."

By the time the 1976 playoff series between the Bruins and Montreal Canadiens rolled around, she was a star. There's no media feeding frenzy quite like a hockey playoff feeding frenzy, and Blue got so much publicity that Montreal coach Scott Bowman felt constrained to point out, without anyone asking, that he too had a dog and he'd be only too glad to reveal its life history to the media, seeing as that was where their interest seemed to lie.

He earned his dog a couple of sidebars but little else.

The story most often associated with Blue came about on the day she nipped Don's wife, Rose. The incident caused considerable concern in the Cherry household – a circumstance that was usually reserved for Don himself – and when Cherry arrived at the rink later in the morning, he was despondent. "What's the matter, Don?" asked Cashman. "You look down."

Cherry told him what had happened.

"Well, that's it," said Cashman. "You'll have to get rid of her now."

"Yeah, I know," said Cherry. "And it's a shame because Rose was a good wife."

• • •

I was in New Jersey one time when Pat Burns was coaching there and needed to talk to him about something. I knew that this might not be as easy as it sounded. The New Jersey franchise under Lou Lamoriello was the NHL's version of the gulag. Even Burns was subject to Lamoriello's authoritarian rules: he was forced to shave off his trademark moustache, thereby making it a former trademark, when he joined the Devils.

Lamoriello does not approve of facial hair on his personnel. It's interesting to note that Canadian penitentiaries allow facial hair on their inmates but the New Jersey Devils don't.

In the arena, there were surveillance cameras to keep an eye on the players – and the media for that matter – in the communal area outside the dressing room. There were strict rules about media access – so strict that in some cases they made a mockery of the NHL rules in that regard (although in fairness, it must be pointed out that when the NHL later devised a new access code, the Devils complied fully).

Attendance at Devils team dinners was mandatory, and no alcoholic beverages were to be served, not even a glass of wine with the main course. Players were required to be dressed identically when they posed for the head-shots in the media guide.

It was in this atmosphere that I managed to get Burns aside for a moment and told him that I needed to talk to him. There was a league-mandated coaches' press conference after the game, but even though I can't remember what it was I needed from Burns, I know it wasn't the kind of thing that I wanted to bring up at a press conference. "Come to my office in five minutes, after the press conference ends," said Burns. "Don't let Lou see you." Under Lamoriello's rules, coaches were not allowed to hold one-on-one discussions with the media wretches.

Needless to say, the coach's office in the arena was not identified. Why would it be? The only people authorized to be there were the coach and the GM, and they both knew where it was. When the time came for the assignation, I knocked briskly on a likely door and walked in. Nice move. It was the wrong door. This was the assistant coaches' room. Clearly, I should have knocked on the other unmarked door, the one that was about fifteen feet farther down the hall.

One of the assistant coaches was Bobby Carpenter, who had a look on his face that was a unique mixture of shock, horror, fear, and amazement. I can't remember the specifics of the look on the face of the other assistant coach, John MacLean, but I do recall that he was equally stunned. A media person had entered their exclusive domain! It would be like a stripper walking into the College of Cardinals. Not knowing that Burns had a separate office, I said, "Is Pat here?"

An adjoining door was open, and on the other side, I now realized, was Burns's office. Having heard my arrival, he shouted, "Come on in." I did. Neither Carpenter nor MacLean had managed to say a word. I went next door. "If Lou catches you in here, there'll be hell to pay," said Burns. "What do you need?"

I got whatever it was; then Burns poked his head out the door to make sure the coast was clear, and I went on my way.

That was typical of Burns. He wasn't kidding about the trouble he would have been in if Lamoriello had discovered my presence in the coach's office.

But because I was a friend and because I needed something, he was willing to take his chances.

• • •

Not long afterwards, the Devils were making a Stanley
Cup run, and the media area underneath the stands was
packed. Long tables had been set up with monitors and
telephones where writers could bang out their pre-game
stories and could even cover the game from there if they
wanted. Sometimes, a paper's deadlines were such that it
made more sense for a reporter to stay down in the base-
ment while the game was being played rather than fight
the crowds getting all the way back down from a fifth-
level press box once the game had ended. Before the game,
that lower media area was always crowded. After all, food
was served in that area as well. Free food.

Before one game, Burns came strolling in and spotted
me as he was walking past the media area on his way to his
office. A coach's presence always attracts attention from
the media. Doubly so when the coach stops. Everyone
looked at him. "Hey, Al," he shouted. "That wasn't right
what you wrote in today's column, you know." He then
proceeded to let everyone know what I had written and
where the mistake was.

There's not much you can do in a situation like that.
He was right, of course. "Yeah, I know," I said. "It dawned
on me later. Do you want a correction?"

"Naw," he said. "I don't care." Then he marched off, his
step a little more jaunty than it had been and with a little
grin on his face. Once again, that was typical Burns – one
of those "gotcha" moments that he enjoyed so much.

• • •

The Hockey Hall of Fame is one of those institutions that is rarely praised. When it selects for induction a player who is a unanimously acclaimed superstar, the decision is greeted with equanimity and labelled a no-brainer.

Every other selection spurs controversy, scepticism, and sometimes outright ridicule.

Even so, the Hockey Hall of Fame rarely received as much acrimony as it did when it announced its 2010 selections and revealed that it had left Pat Burns off the list. By that time, everyone knew that Burns was terminally ill and that the cancer he had beaten twice before was finally going to take his life. He had survived colon cancer in 2004 and liver cancer in 2005. This time, the colon cancer had returned and spread to his lungs.

He had made what was expected to be his last public appearance in March at the press conference announcing that the Pat Burns Arena was to be built in Stanstead, Quebec, about 150 kilometres southeast of Montreal.

It was widely assumed at that time that in light of the fact that he had been named the NHL's coach of the year no fewer than three times and had coached the Devils to the Stanley Cup, the Hall of Fame would honour him and that he would be able to stay alive until the November induction.

Five people were selected for the 2010 induction: two women, Angela James and Cammi Granato, who had represented Canada and the United States respectively in the Olympics; a general manager, Jimmy Devellano; an owner, the late Daryl Seaman; and a player, Dino Ciccarelli. But not a coach. Not Pat Burns. This elicited a huge backlash against the Hall. Burns's many friends and admirers demanded to know how he could be overlooked. Everyone knew that Burns wouldn't live until the 2011 induction. If he was going to accept the honour in person, it had to be done in 2010.

When the inductions themselves took place on Novomber 8, the controversy flared up again. Burns had survived that long but he was not being honoured. Once more the Hall's selection committee was excoriated.

When Burns died on November 19, the abuse started for a third time.

And when the memorial service was held at Montreal's Marie Reine de la Monde Cathedral on November 29 and was attended by a host of hockey's biggest names, the Hall suffered a fourth lambasting in the public forums. The selectors were vilified as idiots and worse. NHL commissioner Gary Bettman was criticized for the non-selection, even though his involvement with the Hall is minimal at best.

The Hall, meanwhile, said nothing of consequence. It couldn't. The rules of selection are strict. The committee members are reminded again and again that they are not to discuss their deliberations and must under no circumstances reveal why they voted, or did not vote, for a specific candidate.

But what happened on that June day when Burns was spurned was really nothing more than confusion. There are certain criteria by which names are put forward and considered. Then, unless a specific percentage of the vote is reached, the name is dropped.

There were some members who, for reasons that had more to do with political correctness than hockey, wanted to make sure that two women got in. And there was considerable confusion about the number of people who could be inducted in any given year. There were those who thought that even if they didn't vote for Burns on an early ballot, they would still be able to do so later.

But when the smoke cleared, Burns was not on the list. Some selectors were stunned and asked for another vote, but as was mentioned earlier, the rules are strict. The voting had followed the prescribed format and was now concluded.

Burns had been left off, and nothing could be done about it.

• • •

It was at the beginning of the 2006–07 season that the National Hockey League made what appeared to be a minor announcement: the duration of TV time outs would be increased by twenty seconds.

It appeared to be a subtle change, one that wouldn't really affect anybody. But it impacted the game far beyond any fan's expectations. At first glance, it doesn't appear that there's much you can do in twenty seconds. After all, in the immortal words of Bobby Hull during his brief stint as a colour man on *Hockey Night in Canada* telecasts, "A second goes by pretty fast."

If you're a sportswriter, you could watch someone else do twenty push-ups. If you're a lawyer, you could carve in stone a list of all the good things your profession has done for society.

But if you're a top-level hockey coach, you can change the face of your game.

The concept of adding twenty seconds to each of the three TV time outs that are mandated for each period was instituted by John Shannon, who, at the time, held the NHL title of senior vice-president for broadcasting.

That's not a reflection on Shannon's ability. He is the best hockey producer in the world even though he has now opted to be on the other side of the camera and works for Sportsnet. Because of his excellence as a producer, he was repeatedly hired by the International Olympic Commission to provide its host feed, and that expertise goes a long way to explaining why he was fired from *Hockey Night in Canada* by Nancy Lee, who, on a good day, knew which end of a camera to point.

When he got to the NHL, Shannon's job was to improve the level of NHL broadcasts, especially those in the United States, and it was his contention that with TV time outs of one minute and forty seconds, fans were not getting to see enough replays of a game's most exciting moments.

After ninety seconds of commercials, only ten seconds remained, and one or two of those seconds were invariably squandered before the commercials started.

By the time one post-commercial replay had been shown, live action had resumed. But as any hockey fan knows, it often helps to see a play from a second or third angle. And sometimes, more than one play deserves a second look.

Broadcasters were having a problem in this area, and it was exacerbated by the fact that the league was in the process of introducing the concept of "hurry-up faceoffs." Broadcasters had been able to take advantage of players who were slow to get to the faceoff spot or linesmen who dawdled and squeeze in a replay or two. But now the league had decreed that these time-wasting practices were to end.

So Shannon added twenty seconds to the break, imposing the condition on the broadcasters that the extra time was not to be used for more commercials. An extra twenty seconds doesn't seem like a big difference. But to a professional coach, it is. Paul Maurice, who has had a number of NHL head-coaching jobs, said flatly, "It's a gold mine."

"It's seems like a very small detail," said Bob Hartley, a Stanley Cup–winning coach, "but that two-minute time out, rather than a minute, or a minute-and-a-half, is a huge difference." The coaches used that full two-minute time out to rest their star players. Then they sent them out again. After the lengthening of the time out, ice time for the league's star players increased in almost every case. "There's nothing wrong with that," said Maurice. "People come to watch these guys play.

"I've always thought that the best players could play a little bit more, that they're more exciting to watch play."

In today's hockey, shifts are usually in the forty second range. Therefore, if the game were to continue, in two minutes of playing time, a coach could send out his second, third, and fourth lines.

In two minutes of a TV time out, he can pretend that those three lines have had their turn. If the first-line players were out before the break, they can go right back out after the break.

Those twenty seconds have changed the nature of coaching. When the TV time outs were shorter, a coach would plan his strategy based on who he would send out after the next time out.

Once the two-minute break was instituted, a coach's plans became based on who he would send out *before* the next time out.

And since the time outs are taken according to a precise schedule – at the stoppages closest to five, ten, and fifteen minutes of each period, with a little variance for power plays – a smart coach can get his stars out much more than he ever did.

But the stars aren't unduly tired because their rest time between shifts hasn't been reduced. And most of them thrive on the extra work.

There's nothing wrong with it from the fans' point of view either. It makes a better game because the stars are having a greater impact and they are indeed more exciting to watch.

All because of twenty seconds.

# CHAPTER TWELVE

*Fortune is the least capricious of deities, and arranges things in the just and rigid system that no one shall be very happy for very long.*

Evelyn Waugh, *When the Going Was Good*

**It is in the hockey fan's nature** to fantasize. He likes to think his team can win the Stanley Cup, his favourite players can win the major trophies, and so on.

That's fine. But at some point, someone has to draw the line between fantasy and reality, and at the moment, in one specific area, it seems that no one is willing to do that.

There is a pervasive theory that before long, another one of the troubled American teams will eagerly load up the moving vans and head to Canada. Some think the new home will be Quebec City. Fans in southern Ontario think that they should be first in line.

The problem is that, for the most part, these are both fantasies.

Could a U.S.–based team move to Canada? Yes it

could. The Atlanta Thrashers did it on May 31, 2011, when they moved to Winnipeg.

Would another move be an easy process? Absolutely not.

There is only one way another American team would relocate north of the border. Every other possible course of action would have been explored to the fullest and proved fruitless.

This is what happened in the case of the Thrashers. If there is one indisputable fact that arose from the Thrashers' move, it is that there was not, at the time, one single human being in the United States who would buy the team and keep it in that country.

NHL commissioner Gary Bettman and the league's board of governors fought tooth and nail every step of the way to prevent a team leaving an American market for Canada. Bettman explored every possible opportunity. He talked to – or dispatched his minions to talk to – every American businessman who might possibly be interested in acquiring an NHL team. He tried hard to work out a deal with the existing owners in Atlanta.

Yet the cupboard was bare.

A new arena in Quebec City will not be ready until 2014 at the earliest, and by that time, it is expected that the economic situation in the United States will have improved.

If that's the case, then Bettman probably will be able to find the one potential investor that he needs – or the one group of investors that will serve the purpose. And it should not be overlooked that in order to move the Thrashers to Winnipeg, the new owners had to give the governors a $60 million "relocation fee" to be shared among the other twenty-nine teams.

There are governors who would prefer to disband a team and distribute its players to the remaining NHL teams through a draft, rather than put another team in Canada.

That's the reality.

•   •   •

Most Canadians don't understand the reluctance of the NHL's governors to expand the league's presence in Canada.

Teams in Quebec City and southern Ontario are something that most Canadians would like to see because we know that we're supporting the league financially right now.

We know that U.S. television ratings are in a funk everywhere and that in some American venues, published attendance figures don't come close to representing the number of people who are actually in the building. We see packed arenas in Canada and strong television support. We know that hockey is our national game and we love it with a passion.

But none of these things matter to the NHL governors, the vast majority of whom are American. And when the decision is made about the relocation of any U.S.–based team, it is not Canadian hockey fans who will make the decision. It is the NHL's board of governors.

For one thing, those governors have not forgotten the relatively recent problems of the Canadian dollar. It bounced back nicely and not only attained par with the American greenback but passed it in value.

When you make a decision about the location of a hockey team, however, you try to look at the long term.

It's an arguable point, but in a resource-based economy such as Canada's, which is steadily reducing its component of skilled workers and managers, the long-term outlook for the dollar is questionable. Even though Canada's gross national product continues to grow, the share that comes from resources is twice what it was five years ago. Will the world continue to demand those resources – our gold, lumber, minerals, and so on, and will they last?

We don't want to debate economic matters in a sports book. But the point must be made that governors look at these things while fans do not. And they're not totally convinced that the Canadian dollar will stay strong.

The governors, naturally enough, also consider the impact on their own team. If, for instance, you own the Los Angeles Kings or Colorado Avalanche, do you want to try to sell tickets based on the fact that Kitchener or Hamilton is coming to town? From their point of view, it's bad enough that they now have to try to sell Winnipeg.

Viewing audiences are market-oriented. No matter how vehemently NHL commissioner Gary Bettman

tries to deny it, the 2006 Stanley Cup final between the
Edmonton Oilers and Carolina Hurricanes was a ratings
disaster.

Two subsequent Stanley Cup finals between the
Detroit Red Wings and Pittsburgh Penguins were far
better. The 2010 final between the Chicago Blackhawks
and Philadelphia Flyers was a bonanza.

To put it in terms the governors understand, if you
put teams in small markets, they make less money for the
league. And Winnipeg, with a population in the 700,000
range, is the smallest market in the NHL.

In theory, a renegade like Jim Balsillie could buy a
struggling American team and move it to Canada despite
league edicts, just as Al Davis flouted the National
Football League's edicts by moving the Oakland Raiders
to Los Angeles.

Balsillie tried such a move with the Phoenix Coyotes
but was unable to pull it off. A lot of legal roadblocks
have been established by professional leagues since Davis
succeeded in that regard. The people in the NHL's New
York office may not know anything about hockey, but
they know about legalities. They know full well how
many headaches Al Davis caused for the NFL, and they
have done everything in their power to make sure that
it's impossible for someone to cause the NHL that kind
of trouble.

If another team is to be moved from the United States
to Canada, it will have to be done with the approval of the

NHL's governors – the guys who own the teams. That will be no easy task.

•  •  •

When the NHL governors consider the location of a team, they ask themselves three questions and like to get positive answers to every single one.

(1) Will a team from that market be likely to draw in my building?
(2) Will that team increase league-wide television revenues?
(3) Will that team be self-sufficient or will it be a perennial drain on the revenue-sharing pool?

In the first case, the answer is a solid "no" where Canadian cities are concerned. It is an unassailable fact that most Americans know or care very little about anything outside their borders. Very few of them could identify Canada's prime minister. Very few of them would know where to place our large cities on a map. Very few have heard of places like Winnipeg, Quebec, and Hamilton.

Americans want to see teams from places like Chicago, New York, and Los Angeles. If they must, they'll show up for Pittsburgh, Dallas, and some others. But if Carolina is a tough sell, which it is, how could any reasonable person – or NHL governor – think that teams from small Canadian markets would help his ticket sales?

On to the second point. *Hockey Night in Canada* is a large contributor to NHL coffers. TSN and Sportsnet also contribute when they show national games, but would network revenues increase if Canada had eight or nine teams instead of the present seven? Not appreciably.

Similarly, revenues will show no appreciable increase as a result of Winnipeg having come back into the fold.

This is the key point. Network revenues are shared league-wide. Local revenues are not.

If Sportsnet shows an Ottawa Senators game on Sportsnet East, that's not a national network game, even though Sportsnet is a national network. Because the Senators are being shown on only a regional segment of the network, the rest of the league would not share in the revenue.

So if the newly transplanted Canadian franchises found local sponsors – as they almost certainly would – and made lots of money from local television, that wouldn't put a penny in the pockets of the governors of the other teams.

So the answer for (2), as it was for (1), is a resounding "no."

On the third point, Canadians like to think that any NHL team within the country's boundaries will be successful. But as American governors will point out – usually not for attribution – Canadian teams have been just as fragile as their American counterparts.

It wasn't that long ago that Canadians were openly expressing their concerns about the future of three Canadian teams: the Edmonton Oilers, Calgary Flames, and Ottawa Senators, all of which were openly seeking financial assistance from the federal government.

The Oilers and Flames, through concerted appeals to civic pride, managed to stay alive. The Ottawa Senators went bankrupt before they could be resuscitated.

There were fears of the Montreal Canadiens being moved to the United States until a benevolent owner – an American of all things – bought them in 2001 and solved the problem after no Canadian purchaser could be found.

The Winnipeg Jets moved to Phoenix in 1996 and became the Coyotes because they were not financially viable in Winnipeg. The Quebec Nordiques moved to Denver in 1995 and became the Colorado Avalanche because they were not financially viable in Quebec.

So the answer to (3) is just as negative as the answers to (1) and (2). Fans are welcome to dream as much as they want about increased Canadian involvement in the NHL. But they shouldn't let fantasy get in the way of reality. The reality is that unless every other possible avenue has been exhausted, American teams are staying where they are.

·   ·   ·

Now those are the reasons, from an American point of view, why the move of another U.S.–based team to Canada would be highly unlikely. But it should not be forgotten that there is a negative side in Canada as well. Canadian hockey fans may have forgotten about the dark era of Canadian teams in the NHL. Or they may never have known about it.

You can be sure, however, that the NHL head office hasn't forgotten, and if the subject of moving more teams to Canada starts to become serious, the governors will receive a remedial history lesson.

At the beginning of the twenty-first century, it was easy to find people who insisted that the days were not far off when Canada would have no more than one or two teams in the NHL. The Canadian dollar was weak. Hockey was in its clutch-and-grab phase. The Canadian teams weren't very competitive. Financial problems were everywhere.

From the depths of the gloom came pleas from some teams, supported by many fans, for federal involvement.

The first step was an attempt by the western teams to set up their own TV network. It would show games involving those teams on a pay-per-view basis and would help them overcome their financial woes.

The CRTC, a government agency that oversees broadcasting in the country, refused to give them a licence, preferring instead to allow a couple of women's networks to be established. One would have been acceptable. But two at the same time when there was no evidence that even one would be supported?

The financial problems persisted for Canadian NHL teams, and some were in real danger of following Winnipeg and Quebec to the United States.

As a result, three teams asked for direct government assistance. The federal government, citing the importance of those teams to Canada, went so far as to approve $10.5 million in grants.

The reaction, especially from the chattering classes in Toronto, was so hysterical that the government reversed its stance and within forty-eight hours withdrew the grants.

As is usually the case in Canada, the overriding emotion driving those who opposed the grants was envy. It wasn't logic. It wasn't passion. It was simply the fact that after living under decades of varying degrees of socialism, Canadians hate nothing as much as a wealthy Canadian.

So when they managed to convince themselves that their tax dollars were going to go to "rich hockey players," they let out such a scream that the Liberal government, which had no principles of its own, only an all-abiding desire to cling to power, did a 180-degree turn and withdrew its offer of funding for Canada's NHL teams.

If Canadians were smart they would have asked themselves the one question that the critics of tax relief for Canadian teams never adequately answered.

What is wrong with giving $3.5 million to get $17 million?

Strip off the peripheral issues and it was really that simple. The federal government was willing to give each

qualifying Canadian team $3.5 million in order to guarantee
that it stayed in Canada. In return, the nation would continue to receive the taxes that those teams paid – in the
typical case, the Ottawa Senators, $17 million in federal
taxes, $37 million at all levels. What was wrong with that?

There were lots of answers to that question, but none
that made sense.

One answer was that money should not be going to
hockey when the country needed more funds for hospitals, health care, and various other concerns.

Yes, but if that $17 million ceased to exist because the
team moved to the United States, wouldn't that mean a
net loss of $14 million for important causes? How would
the hospitals be better off with $14 million less?

Another common answer was that the NHL should
first clean up its own house. That may be so, but it was
a completely different issue. It had nothing to do with
the question at hand. What was wrong with giving out
$3.5 million to get $17 million?

Then there were suggestions that NHL players are all
so rich, they should not receive handouts. That was the
Canadian envy coming to the fore. We would rather miss
out on the $17 million than see any wealthy Canadian
do well.

It was a stupid argument because hockey players were
not going to get any less money once they were forced out
of Canada. In fact, they would get more money because
American taxes aren't as onerous as Canadian.

So by refusing to give the teams the grants, the federal government was, in fact, creating an opportunity for the rich to get richer. The only difference would be that this time, when they paid their taxes, the players would send their money to Washington, not to Ottawa.

The owners of American NHL teams are not exactly fervent supporters of government interference. But they like to think that if they need government support, they can get it. The lesson that they learned back in that dark era was that in Canada, that's not the case.

And it's one more reason that a further increase in the number of Canadian teams is unlikely.

•   •   •

If anyone doubts how fanatically the NHL will fight to keep an established team in the United States, look at what happened in Phoenix.

The NHL first did battle with Jim Balsillie, who wanted to move the Coyotes to southern Ontario.

It then took over ownership of the team and assumed its losses for a year while trying unsuccessfully to line up a new owner. In the interim, it went toe to toe with the Goldwater Institute, a watchdog organization dedicated to minimizing government spending.

The NHL pressured the Glendale city council to the point that on May 10, 2011, it accepted a deal that cost the taxpayers $25 million but kept the Coyotes in

Phoenix (actually the suburb of Glendale) for another year.

That meeting was attended by both Bettman and the NHL's deputy commissioner, Bill Daly.

In the preceding weeks, the news media had been full of stories asserting that the Coyotes' move to Winnipeg was a *fait accompli*. Some stories even predicted the date of the announcement.

Dave Tippett, the coach of the Coyotes, was furious when a Sportsnet story insisted on the eve of the playoffs that the Coyotes would be moved to Winnipeg as soon as they were eliminated. He saw it as a distraction that damaged his team's chances, and when the Coyotes got swept by the Detroit Red Wings, it was hard to argue with him.

With the sweep, the proposed date for the move arrived. The Coyotes stayed put.

•  •  •

As soon as the transfer of the Phoenix franchise was ruled out, a chorus arose predicting the immediate move of the Atlanta Thrashers to Winnipeg.

I'm certainly not going to suggest that there hadn't already been attempts made in that regard. In fact, I was the one who first broke the story – on *Hockey Night in Canada* in October 2009.

Even that long ago, Canadian billionaire David Thomson, one of the eventual partners in the group that

now owns the Winnipeg franchise, was laying the groundwork for the deal.

His biggest problem came from within. The Thrashers'
owners were at each other's throats and Thomson couldn't
find a compromise that would satisfy all the parties.

On May 10, 2011, when the Coyotes' immediate
future was determined, the Thrashers deal was still a long
way from being done, even though a number of news
outlets – even the *Globe and Mail* – ran stories saying
all the arrangements had been made. That was simply
not the case.

The NHL was still fighting the move with all the
resolve it could muster, and a frantic search was under
way to find a buyer who would keep the team in Atlanta.

Thrashers co-owner Michael Gearon made no secret
of that fact. "I've been focused on trying to avoid this
day," he said when the move finally came about. "I spent
time with possible investors going back four years ago,
because I was concerned this day would come. I made a
desperate plea in February. Unfortunately, that didn't lead
to any real prospects. To be sitting here today is just awful
for me."

With no American saviours having been found, the
team's transfer took place, but even then, not until the
lawyers had done battle in an all-night meeting so that
the deal could be announced before the Stanley Cup final
kicked off the following night.

• • •

Canadians were jubilant at the return of a franchise, and so they should have been. But a close examination of the deal should induce at least a degree of caution, if not outright scepticism.

The analogy might be made of a child who gets a new puppy. He promises to clean up after it, to feed it, and to walk it. But before long, the lustre wears off and the adults get stuck with all the chores.

Even NHL commissioner Gary Bettman tempered his enthusiasm for the move. "We don't like to move a franchise," he said. "We're not happy about leaving Atlanta. This was never about whether Winnipeg is better than Atlanta. The decision to come to Winnipeg was only made after the Atlanta ownership made the decision they were going to sell even if it meant the club was going to leave Atlanta."

The move was conditional upon the Winnipeg franchise being able to sell 13,000 season tickets with three-year commitments in three weeks.

Given the fact that the tickets would be among the third-highest in Canada after Toronto and Montreal – and eighth-highest in the entire NHL – and that Winnipeg had just become the NHL's smallest market, the new franchise appeared to be facing a monumental challenge.

However, the tickets sold out in a few minutes. The alacrity with which they disappeared was something of a surprise, but the fact that they sold wasn't. Clearly, in Winnipeg, supporting an NHL team was the thing to do.

The bigger problem is looming down the road. It's one thing to line up for tickets when you know that by doing so, you're contributing to the return of an NHL team to your community. But are you going to line up again five years later when the gun is no longer at your head?

Bettman, who usually dances around such issues, didn't do so this time. "To be candid, this isn't going to work very well unless this building is sold out every night," he said.

Those of us who remember the apathetic approach of fans when the Jets' demise was imminent have some concerns, even though we hope they're unfounded.

• • •

The size of the MTS Arena in Winnipeg is another problem. It seats only 15,015, the lowest capacity in the league.

The United Center in Chicago, for instance, seats 19,717. Capacity in Montreal is 21,273. Even in Detroit's Joe Louis Arena, one of the oldest buildings in the league, capacity is 20,066.

With so few seats available, Winnipeg's margin for error is smaller. If the team were to have a poor crowd one night, it wouldn't be able to compensate by selling 20,000 seats the next night. On the bright side, Winnipeg inherited a good team, one that could be expected to make the playoffs in its first season as long as it could overcome its travel difficulties.

Because the franchise was to remain in the Southeast Division, it would have to make frequent trips to the Eastern Seaboard of the United States – to Miami, Tampa, Washington, and Carolina. Even so, the team's travel woes would be no worse than most of those in the NHL's Western Conference.

As a result, the Thrashers' move gave Winnipeg fans a second crack at supporting an NHL team. Canadians fervently hope they'll do so, and they probably will. But the challenge should not be underestimated.

# CHAPTER THIRTEEN

*Life is not mathematics, and few things have only one answer.*

Allan Massie, *The Evening of the World*

**Every spring,** after the Toronto Maple Leafs have stumbled through the season with the usual predictable result, their many fans are faced with a difficult decision: Who should they support now? It's the playoffs, the best time of the season, and the only way to see the Leafs is to take up golf.

Most Leafs fans can't bring themselves to cheer for the hated Montreal Canadiens. Or any team in the Leafs' division. Those teams are, by definition, divisional rivals, presumably the teams you hate the most.

The best idea for Leafs fans? Switch your allegiance to the team that, after the Leafs, you financially support the most. As often as not, that's the Nashville Predators.

In the NHL that Gary Bettman built, the idea prevails that if you build a strong team, you get punished.

You see it every year. In the 2010–11 season, it was the once-resurgent Chicago Blackhawks who had to unload a host of quality players in order to keep the team's payroll under the salary cap. Thanks to the combination of the salary cap and revenue-sharing, the National Hockey League's successful teams are penalized.

And from a financial point of view, no team is stronger than the Toronto Maple Leafs. So the Leafs invariably get dinged the most under the revenue-sharing – something in the neighbourhood of $10–12 million U.S. in recent years.

The team that often takes the most from the revenue-sharing program is Nashville. The Predators, it seems, are to the NHL what Quebec is to Canada.

League officials insist that the precise numbers attached to these endowments have to be kept secret. Presumably, this is a decision made out of embarrassment.

In the new NHL, the economic considerations are far more important than the hockey considerations. Trades are based on contracts, not ability, and rosters are determined not by the players you can attract but by the players the league allows you to pay.

So the details of the revenue-sharing, which is an integral part of the economics of the NHL, should also be shared with the fans. But the league won't do it. Requests for the figures are turned down.

In simple terms, the revenue-sharing concept rewards failure, and the subsidies are based on three primary factors: the money a team makes, the money it spends, and the size of its market. That last qualification was put in there to prevent revenue-sharing going to what at the time was a bunch of dysfunctional bumblers in Chicago. And it is somewhat ironic that the Hawks – which were once singled out because they were expected to be at the lower end, have now been singled out because they are at the top end.

It was not until Bill Wirtz died in 2007, taking his nineteenth-century approach to the game with him, that hockey became popular in Chicago again.

But until that time, no home games were shown on television and marketing of the Blackhawks was almost non-existent. Even in the NHL, a league that loves to reward ineptitude, the Hawks had gone too far and the governors wanted to make sure that Wirtz didn't collect what was supposed to be a fund to help out the league's less-advantaged members.

If your team is in a city the size of Chicago, the governors reasoned, you're simply excluded from the plan on the grounds that if your revenues are in the lower third, it's your own fault.

To collect on the revenue-sharing, the team has to be in the bottom half of the league in revenue. Almost without exception, the Toronto Maple Leafs are Number 1.

The number of television households in your market has to be below 2.5 million (another anti-Chicago rule). Also, you have to be in the bottom half of the team payroll list. The numbers are collated, and the top third pays out what the bottom third collects. The middle third drools with envy and tries to figure out a way to cut payrolls. Or cut ticket prices to reduce revenues and therefore qualify for assistance. It's a strange system.

And the curious part is that one of the league's most consistent on-ice failures, the Toronto Maple Leafs franchise, is the one that shells out the most.

•  •  •

Every long-time fan of the Toronto Maple Leafs remembers *the* trade. It was the one with the Calgary Flames for Doug Gilmour, a major turning point in the team's fortunes.

The fans also know that the deal was made by Leafs general manager Cliff Fletcher, who is universally praised for his actions.

What is not as widely known is that when Fletcher started working on the trade, he was trying to get rid of Gilmour, not acquire him.

Before he joined the Leafs, Fletcher was the GM of the Calgary Flames and Gilmour was on his roster. Although he liked Gilmour as a player, there were some other issues, mostly financial, that encouraged Fletcher to consider a parting of the ways.

As a result, he tried to get Leafs' GM Floyd Smith to make a deal that was built around sending Gilmour to Toronto for Gary Leeman – with some extra players thrown in. Smith was receptive to the idea, but the two could never come to an agreement.

The next year, Fletcher took over from Smith and renewed the talks, this time with Doug Risebrough, who had succeeded him as GM of the Flames. As Fletcher's assistant in Calgary, Risebrough had been involved in all the earlier negotiations.

The tipping point was an arbitrator's decision. Gilmour had been unhappy with the Flames' offer for a new contract and had elected to take his case to arbitration.

He was awarded $750,000, which didn't match his true value, as any serious hockey fan would know. But arbitrators aren't hockey fans, they're arbitrators. (In the middle of a hearing, one once asked, "What's this five-on-five you guys are always talking about?")

Gilmour asked Risebrough to exceed the amount the arbitrator had awarded, and when Risebrough refused, Gilmour left the team.

Fletcher was quick to get on the phone to Risebrough, and by the time the two finished, a ten-player trade, the largest in NHL history, had been arranged.

The Leafs sent Leeman, Michel Petit (famously described by a former coach, Bob McCammon, as having "all the tools but no toolbox"), Alexander Godynyuk, Craig Berube, and Jeff Reese to Calgary. In return they got Gilmour, Jamie Macoun, Ric Nattress, Kent Manderville, and Rick Wamsley.

None of the players sent to the Flames did an awful lot. Gilmour, meanwhile, won the Selke Trophy in 1992–93 as the NHL's best defensive forward and finished second to

Mario Lemieux in the voting for the Hart Trophy as the league's MVP. And he set Leafs franchise records for the most points in a season (127) and most assists in a season (95).

And Cliff Fletcher rarely mentioned the fact that he had been willing to trade him for Gary Leeman.

●  ●  ●

During my last run on the "Hotstove" panel, I only heard from Scott Moore once – until the day he fired me because a book I had written referred to me on the cover as being, "from *Hockey Night in Canada*."

The book was *Why the Leafs Suck and How They Can Be Fixed*. Had the book been *Why the Panthers Suck and How They Can Be Fixed*, I'd probably still be on the show.

Moore was the head of CBC Sports at the time of our first encounter, and I had created a bit of turmoil by pointing out the dysfunction in the Tampa Bay Lightning organization.

The two owners were at odds with each other; the players were unhappy, and the coach, Barry Melrose, had been recruited out of the ESPN studios.

I also said that one of the owners, former NHL player Len Barrie, had been in the dressing room drawing up plays and that the over-under on Melrose's tenure was November 15. All of this infuriated the Tampa organization and they made no secret of their displeasure.

Bill Houston, who was writing his "Truth and

Rumours" column in the *Globe and Mail*, called me for a comment, and I told him that the purpose of "Hotstove" was to pass along the gossip and rumours that were going around in the NHL, and that I'd done just that.

That was when Moore called. He was somewhat concerned about the Tampa story, he said, but his greatest concern was that I'd told Houston we dealt in rumours and gossip. "There is no gossip on the CBC," he said. "That's what makes me the most angry. You should never imply that we allow any gossip on the network. The CBC deals in facts, never gossip."

The "Hotstove" segments are available on the CBC website, so I called it up to take another look at what I had said. There, under "Hotstove" on the CBC website, was the corporation's description of the segment. It dealt, the site said, "with rumours and gossip."

Barry Melrose was fired on November 14. That's a fact.

• • •

The off-ice segment of the NHL is no different than any large company. It has capable people. It has dedicated people. It has people on their way up and people on their way down.

It has people who hold positions only because they travel in the right circles and stroke the right executives. It has egomaniacs and meddlers.

But fans like to think that everything is done in an efficient fashion by efficient people. When a fan hears that a key executive has been fired, he tends to believe that a lot of study went into the matter and that the decision was part of a carefully researched long-range plan.

Not necessarily. Often – more often than you'd care to believe – decisions are made on the spur of the moment and implemented on a whim.

There are many of these cases, but a classic example occurred when Mike Keenan was fired as general manager of the Florida Panthers in 2006. The fact that the Panthers have had nine general managers in the eighteen years of their existence tells you a lot about the level of long-term planning in this organization. But it doesn't tell the whole story.

At the time, the Panthers were owned by Alan Cohen, who became an owner when he was lured into "an invest-ment" by Bettman and who may, on a good day, understand the difference between intentional icing and chocolate icing.

Cohen hired Jacques Martin to coach and gave him a five-year deal, even though anyone with a hockey mind knows that coaches rarely last five years.

The first year of Martin's tenure was the lockout. In the second, the Panthers struggled mightily.

But one of the benefits (for the owners) of the lockout was revenue-sharing. Cohen wanted to qualify for it, and to make sure he did, he wouldn't let Keenan spend any serious money to improve the team.

Martin wanted to play defensive hockey, which isn't likely to sell in a market like Florida, and Keenan wanted to fire him. But when the coach has worked only two years of an owner-provided five-year contract, that isn't going to happen. That would make the owner look stupid, and we couldn't have that.

Some of Keenan's players loved him. Some of his players hated him. As Brett Hull once said in his usual cryptic fashion: "Mike Keenan is the kind of guy who will stab you in the back right to your face."

Keenan has been called many names over the years, ranging from "genius" to "complete idiot."

Despite all this, Keenan has never been called "lackadaisical." It is not his nature to sit back and stew in silence. He let Cohen know of his concerns.

His only world-class player was goaltender Roberto Luongo, who told Keenan that he would sign a long-term deal with the club only if he were convinced that there was a commitment from ownership to build a winning team.

The owner would make no such commitment so Keenan had to make the only sensible move. There are still those who criticize him as "the guy who traded Roberto Luongo," but it was that or lose him to free agency.

At the same time, Cohen's son was socializing with some of the players. When hockey players start to travel in the same circles as rich kids, the results are rarely good. It got to the point that Keenan told Cohen that he wanted to win and in order to do so, he needed cooperation. He needed spending. He needed a new coach. He needed some control over dressing-room access.

It was clear that the two men couldn't co-exist and one of them had to go. It wasn't going to be the owner.

Before the meeting, Keenan had a job. After the meeting, he didn't. So much for research and long-term planning. The subsequent announcement said that Keenan had resigned. The new general manager? It was Jacques Martin.

In hockey today, the evidence is overwhelming that one man can't handle the double duties of coach and GM.

But if it saves a salary . . .

•   •   •

Here's another story that challenges the assumption that in the National Hockey League, all major decisions are pre-ceded by lengthy, intense research. Sometimes, hunches supersede reason, and research is replaced by circumstance.

In 1993, the Detroit Red Wings organization decided that the dual role of coach and general manager was too demanding for Bryan Murray. In fact, it's too demanding for anybody, but every so often, a team decides to have one man do both jobs anyway.

That aside, Red Wings senior vice-president Jimmy Devellano went off in search of a coach. It was part of the job description that he had to follow up on any whim that might strike team owner Mike Ilitch.

The guy he targeted was Al Arbour, who, at that point, had been coaching the New York Islanders on and off for the best part of twenty years.

The Islanders were playing the Pittsburgh Penguins, so Jimmy D flew down to the game and approached Arbour with an offer. He could coach the Red Wings on a lucrative long-term contract.

Arbour said that while he was honoured, he was planning to retire to Florida soon – which he did the following season – and he didn't want to undertake a new career with a different team.

Not wanting to waste the trip, Devellano went over to see the coach of the other team. That happened to be Scott Bowman.

Perhaps he would be interested in accepting the offer Arbour had turned down.

He would indeed. Bowman then coached the Wings to three Stanley Cups.

•  •  •

A lot of people don't like Don Cherry. I'm not one of them. Don is a good friend of mine and I think that if the rest of the country acted more like Don Cherry, we'd have a lot fewer problems.

In fact, I think it's a travesty that Don Cherry is not in the Hall of Fame. I'm not going to use as justification the fact that the builders' wing is full of criminals and miscreants, not to mention a host of people who did nothing more for hockey than profit from it. Past errors by the Hall of Fame selection committee are not a good reason to make more errors.

Don deserves to be there for what he has done for the game and continues to do for it.

Whether the country's left-wing media (a redundancy, I know) like it or not – and they don't – Don Cherry is probably the best-known Canadian. Whenever he appears in public, he is mobbed by supporters. The Canadian media don't like Cherry, but the Canadian people certainly do.

He promotes not only NHL hockey but youth hockey. Most nights, he and his son Tim are at junior or midget games. He coaches one of the teams in the annual prospects game, in which the country's best junior players showcase their talents.

Hall of Fame induction is supposed to go to those who promote and build the game. Who does more of that than Don Cherry?

He has his weekly forum on *Hockey Night in Canada*, which he always aims at the hockey-playing youth of the country.

Don tells kids to stand up for their teammates. That can't be bad, can it?

Don tells youngsters to play a clean game. It might be rough. Hockey always has been, and if they didn't know that when they got into the game, it has no doubt become apparent over the years. But being rough doesn't mean being dirty.

Don says you shouldn't attack people from behind and you shouldn't intentionally try to hurt them. Is that wrong?

Don stands up for our armed forces. He is criticized for it, but he does it anyway. Some of his media critics say he does it to get attention. That's ridiculous. Don gets plenty of attention without doing something like that. If there's one thing he does not crave, it's more attention.

And if you believe Don is being phoney, you've never met him. Many people ask me what Don Cherry is really like. I say, "Watch him on Saturday and find out."

Don doesn't put on an act. What you see on Saturday is what you'll see the rest of the week.

He has been one of the leading proponents of making the game safer. He was one of the first to demand shoulder and elbow pads that are themselves padded and cannot be used as weapons, a move that the NHL finally made some five years later.

He has spoken out against the seamless glass that leads to concussions and which many teams installed without considering its effect upon players.

He has been a constant and loud (of course) proponent of no-touch icing, citing the number of players who have been severely injured chasing down relatively unimportant icing calls.

Don says not to embarrass your opponents, to be a gracious winner. No hockey player likes to lose, but everyone does at some point. To lose to a better opponent is acceptable. To be ridiculed for it is not.

For the most part, Don represents the kind of qualities that permeate hockey. These qualities are handed down from generation to generation. You accept authority in your coach and you always do your best.

All these aspects of the game – all its better qualities – are promoted every Saturday by Don Cherry. So is the game itself.

If Don Cherry doesn't belong in the Hall of Fame, who does?

•   •   •

When he was a player, Wayne Gretzky was also one of the of the game's great thinkers. He was never short of ideas for improving the game or making it into a better spectacle for the fans, and once his own kids started to play hockey, Gretzky came up with a few more ideas. Naturally enough, coming from someone like Gretzky, they make a lot of sense. But with the minor-hockey bureaucracy being what it is, they have never caught on.

He doesn't think the NHL should tamper with the size of its nets. But he thinks minor hockey should. "We should make the nets smaller for kids," he says. "In minor league baseball, the distance around the base paths is shorter and the kids use smaller balls. In little league football, they use a smaller ball."

Gretzky's two oldest sons, Ty and Trevor, both played minor hockey, but neither decided to follow in his father's footsteps.

Ty, who was a forward, had great skills and could literally skate before he could walk. As a toddler, he used to zoom around the house on roller blades. But when the time came to decide whether he wanted to make a career of the game, he understandably didn't want to leave his California home to play junior hockey in Canada.

"I wish I could have been able to skate like Ty," Gretzky once said. "I'd really have been something."

Trevor was a goaltender but found he didn't care that much for hockey. He preferred baseball and football and gravitated into baseball's version of the goalie. He's a catcher. In high school, he also played quarterback for his high-school football team (Joe Montana's son was the team's other quarterback), but Trevor opted for baseball after he suffered a separated shoulder.

As of this writing, he's one of the top catchers for his age in southern California, a breeding ground for professional baseball players. The chances are good that we'll see Trevor Gretzky in baseball's major leagues some day.

Wayne used to watch his sons play hockey and said, "We should make our nets smaller for the kids up to the age of twelve. Why should my son use the same puck I use? Why should my son, who's a goaltender, use the same net as Mike Richter? They should use smaller nets and a lighter puck. It would be better for the game."

Gretzky felt that the net, "instead of four feet by six feet, should be three feet by five feet for kids. The puck should be an ounce or two lighter. With the smaller nets, the kids would have more fun and the puck would be smaller so they could shoot it harder."

•  •  •

In another area, Gretzky believes that the biggest factor in youth development is to make sure that whatever size the pucks might be, the kids get to use them.

He was watching a kids practice near his California home one day and was amazed. "I was sitting there with my brother-in-law and said, 'Wow, these kids are ten years old.' I was really impressed. These are ten-year-olds in L.A. and they were flying around and around, backward and forward. I thought, 'There's something wrong here. I don't know what it is, but there's something wrong.'

"Then they threw a puck out and the pace dropped by 50 per cent."

And that, in a nutshell, is one of the problems facing the North American game, says Gretzky. Hockey, by definition, uses a puck. But much of a standard hockey practice doesn't. "The Europeans, every drill they do, they do with the puck," Gretzky says. "With the majority of our kids, as soon as the coaches come on the ice, they put the pucks away. When it comes time to handle the puck at full speed, the kids can't do it.

"That's the one thing that our youth hockey lacks compared to the fifties, sixties, and seventies. When we were kids, we'd go out to the pond or the river or the rink, and the first thing we did was get out a puck. Everybody wanted to carry a puck.

"Nowadays, if you get fifteen or twenty kids and say, 'Okay we're going to play five-a-side pond hockey. Change when you're tired,' I'll bet you 90 per cent of the kids would say, 'What position do you want me to play?' They don't just go. We used to just go. Now, everything has to be so organized for these kids. They don't know what to do. That's what a guy like Paul Kariya did so well. He did everything at the same speed, and that's hard to do."

A guy with a couple of nines on his back also did it pretty well.

•   •   •

Gretzky is not a big proponent of weight training either.

When he was shattering records as a young player, he used to point out that he hadn't been able to manage a third chin-up at the Edmonton Oilers' pre-season testing.

After he retired, he often put it another way: "When I could only do ten sit-ups, I scored ninety goals," he said. "When I could do ninety sit-ups, I scored ten goals."

His buddy Brett Hull took a similar approach.

In September 1991, when his St. Louis Blues were going through their pre-season medicals – a process Hull

loathed – a doctor had him raising his hands above his
head and wasn't overly excited by Hull's efforts. "Is that
the best you can do?" the doctor asked.

"It should be good enough," said Hull. "I managed to
do it eighty-six times last season with no problem."

•  •  •

Hockey players, who are forever in search of sources of
merriment, like to make fun of Kyle Wellwood's tiny
stick. If it's not the shortest in the National Hockey
League, it's awfully close to it.

Tongue depressors with the name WELLWOOD
written on them have been known to find their way onto
the stick rack.

Teammates also make fun of his shot, suggesting that
it's best taken early in the period, otherwise the accumulated snow will prevent the puck from getting to the net.
But those kinds of comments are only made in jest. In
reality, Wellwood's colleagues know that he is a superb
puck-handler and one of the best in the league – whichever league he may be in.

It's hard to think of a player who has had more ups
and downs than Wellwood over the last few years. He
made the Toronto Maple Leafs out of training camp
in 2005 and was hailed as a potential star. At times,
his stick-handling was dazzling and he lived up to
that billing.

At other times, he was excoriated for being lazy and lackadaisical.

He's one of those guys who, to use the time-honoured hockey saying, could stick-handle in a phone booth. But his commitment to the defensive side of the game often appeared to be lacking.

He missed only one game in his first season with the Leafs, but in his second season, he was in and out of the lineup.

After his third season, Wellwood's stock had fallen so low that the Leafs didn't even try to trade him. They simply placed him on waivers. The Vancouver Canucks, rebuilding under new general manager Mike Gillis, picked him up. Again, there were moments when he was a hero and moments when he was a stiff. He lasted a couple of years in Vancouver before he was again released outright.

It appeared that Wellwood had hit rock bottom and was on the exit ramp from professional hockey. The following autumn, he went to the Phoenix Coyotes' training camp. He didn't make the team.

His next destination was Atlant Oblast, a Moscow-based team in the Kontinental Hockey League. Three months later, in January 2011, he was released from Atlant. His fiancée was pregnant – with a child she had in March – and the pair returned to Canada.

That was when the St. Louis Blues signed him. But even that didn't work out. NHL rules require that a player returning from the KHL in mid-season must clear waivers.

Even though the San Jose Sharks were a much better team than the Blues – and proved that point as the season progressed – they were behind the Blues in the standings at the time and therefore able to enter a claim.

Wellwood was only too happy to sign with the Sharks. He was not only back in the NHL, he was on a dynamic line with Joe Pavelski and playing some of his best hockey.

By the end of the season, he was an integral part of the Sharks' attack and once again established as an NHL player.

•  •  •

Like most players, Wellwood grew up using a wooden stick, and there was speculation that when wooden sticks disappeared, Wellwood's stickhandling skills would go with them.

As I noted earlier, composite sticks provide a booming shot, but they make it very difficult to take a pass or to control the puck.

Wellwood may have found the perfect compromise. "What I do is I practise with it," he explained. "I shoot a lot of pucks off the boards to the stick so the blade softens up."

He does it again and again with a bunch of sticks so that he never has to go into a game with a new composite stick. "I wouldn't take a new stick into a game," he says flatly. "I've got a whole bunch ready."

Anyone who has watched him can see why he likes

a short stick. He gets the puck in near his feet, then moves it and dances around it, using his body to keep the puck out of defenders' reach. Sometimes, when he's in action, he looks more like a soccer player than a hockey player.

"I like to make plays when the puck is around my feet," he said. "I like to get in real tight to the defenceman. If I'm close to the D-man, if he's going to fish for it, he's standing still. Then it's easier to make a pass."

In the early stages of Wayne Gretzky's career, when he used a Titan stick made of wood, he used to shorten his stick as the season went on. Every month or so, he'd chop off another half-inch, the theory being that as the season progressed, he became increasingly comfortable with his puck handling.

It is, after all, more difficult to handle a puck that's at your feet rather than one that's out in front of you. But for the game itself, Wellwood keeps his stick at a constant length. He senses that length. He doesn't have to measure it.

As for whether it's the shortest in the league or not, he thinks that Tomas Holmstrom of the Detroit Red Wings might use one of a similar length, but he's not certain. "It's definitely shorter than usual," Wellwood said.

Naturally, a short stick has its drawbacks. If it didn't, everybody would use one.

"The negatives are in puck battles in the corner," Wellwood said. "If the D-man steals it from you, you can't reach and go get it again. That's the drawback. You've really got to be safe with the pass."

Where he's playing makes a difference too.

When he was asked about it during the 2011 playoffs, he said, "I've moved to a stick that's a bit longer because with the Sharks, I'm a winger and there's more emphasis on holding on to the puck in the corner and things like that."

But during the season, when he was called upon to take part in a shootout, he went back to the old tried and true favourite.

"I find it easier to move your body from side to side with a smaller stick," he said.

# CHAPTER FOURTEEN

*I knew that on newspapers, the universal motto, although nobody might ever admit it, was: The worse it gets, the better I like it.*

Gordon Burn, *Fullalove*

**At every meeting of the NHL** general managers, alterations to the rules are discussed. One proposal that was on the verge of becoming a new rule unfortunately fell between the cracks when the focus switched to head shots and supplementary discipline.

It was one of those proposals aimed at reducing the number of stoppages in the game, which is always desirable. The rule would have discouraged goalies from freezing a puck that had been shot in from outside the blue line.

What often happens on long shots at the moment is that the goalie will stop the puck and let it sit at his feet. There is already a rule that prevents him from freezing the puck when no attacker is within range, so he waits until an opposing forward gets close, then he falls on the puck or covers it with his glove.

Fans want to see action, not faceoffs. If the original shot comes from outside the blue line, the netminder has plenty of time to play it. He should be forced to do so.

Although the proposal hasn't become a rule yet, there is a lot of sentiment in favour of it.

•  •  •

Calgary Flames coach Darryl Sutter was clearly not impressed with fighting majors being handed out to his goalie Phillipe Sauve and Colorado goalie David Aebischer after they decided to fight but ended up doing nothing more than exchange hugs. Said Sutter, "They could have given them two minutes for wiping mascara off or something like that."

•  •  •

Fans like to blame the NHL's New York office for everything that goes wrong with the game. They assume that the way the league is run is determined by the people at 1185 Avenue of the Americas.

To a degree, that's true. If the matter is straightforward, that's where the decision will be made. But if it's a matter that has legal ramifications – and given the mindset of the people in the NHL head office, that's pretty well everything that comes up – the decision is made elsewhere.

The NHL head-office people pick up the phone and

dial 212-969-3000, the number for Proskauer Rose LLP.

When you get right down to it, it is not commissioner Gary Bettman, the man with the nice big corner office, who runs the NHL. It's the lawyers over at Proskauer Rose, an expensive (some would say obscenely expensive) legal firm over near Times Square. Bettman and his staff can do the groundwork, but in any matter of consequence, Proskauer Rose has the final say.

When the league needs extra help during its many confrontations with its workers, in comes Bob Batterman – a partner at Proskauer Rose.

When Bettman decided that he wanted to investigate the vastly overblown "gambling scandal," involving Janet Gretzky and Rick Tocchet, he quickly made it clear that he had more faith in Proskauer Rose than in Wayne Gretzky. He brought in one of the Proskauer Rose lawyers, Robert Cleary, to do the investigation.

Bettman stressed to the media that he had the utmost faith that Cleary would act with impeccable integrity, a quality he at no time attributed to Wayne Gretzky.

Whenever an NHL team is sold, or makes any changes in the corporate structure, copies of the agreement go to the league's legal staff and to Proskauer Rose.

When the NHL lost its ESPN TV deal after the lockout, the man on the front lines for the negotiation with the Outdoor Life Network was Doug Perlman, who held the curious title of executive vice-president, media. He was a former associate at Proskauer Rose.

The Outdoor Life Network subsequently changed its named to Versus in the United States – but it still remained nearly invisible, as it had when it was the Outdoor Life Network.

When he was asked about the laughable NHL TV situation at the time, Perlman said, "We're certainly going to try to grow ratings. I certainly wouldn't say we need to, but it's a key metric that people measure the popularity of the sport by, so we're certainly focused on it."

Other than the fact that Perlman has an affinity for "certainly," what we were left to deduce from this was that ratings don't matter. This is not a view shared by Bettman, and Perlman moved on shortly afterwards.

Coincidentally enough, before getting into the sports world, Bettman worked at Proskauer Rose.

•  •  •

Although there is the occasional exception, the general rule for NHL coaches is that they are required to meet the media on a daily basis.

They're also required to meet the media after each game.

Coaches tend to fall into three categories when it comes to dealing with the media.

Some of them accept the chore readily and make the most of the opportunity to follow their own personal agenda. They can complain about the officiating, criticize aspects of their team's performance, praise individual players, or just wax philosophical about the sport.

Some coaches hate dealing with the media but hide it well. The prototype of this species was Pat Quinn, who would gladly have spent the rest of his life without ever saying another word into a microphone or tape recorder. Nevertheless, he was an excellent interview. He always gave thoughtful, insightful answers, even though in many cases the questions didn't warrant it.

The third type of coach is the one who hates dealing with the media and makes no secret of it. Did someone say John Tortorella?

He is the coach of the New York Rangers these days, after having been fired by the Tampa Bay Lightning. In between jobs, he did a spell on TSN, where he himself had a media job. He was just as grumpy with the other guys on the panel when he was on TV as he is with the media when he's coaching.

His primary antagonist is Larry Brooks, veteran hockey columnist of the *New York Post*. Brooks was a writer in the seventies, then went to the dark side as a PR man for the New Jersey Devils. If you watch that faded but famous clip of Jim Schoenfeld calling referee Don Koharski a fat pig, that's Brooks in his seventies haircut (even though it was the eighties) shepherding Schoenfeld away.

Brooks saw the light, went back to journalism and covers the Rangers on a daily basis. And he does battle with Tortorella on an almost daily basis.

To set the stage, on the final weekend of the 2010–11 season, the Rangers squeaked into the playoffs. They lost to the Devils, but the Carolina Hurricanes couldn't defeat the Tampa Bay Lightning to get the two points they needed to grab eighth place and eliminate New York.

The Rangers lost the first game of the playoffs to the Washington Capitals; then, on the morning of the second game, Tortorella showed up for the mandatory press conference.

Brooks: Do you think going into this game that your backs are against the wall?

Tortorella: Do I think our backs are against the wall? This is a series.

Brooks: That's what I'm asking. Are your backs against the wall right now?

Tortorella: I never think our backs are against the walls. In a series . . .

Brooks: In a series or any time?

Tortorella: Any time.

Brooks: So you didn't think your backs were against the wall Saturday?

Tortorella: Saturday?

Brooks: Against New Jersey?

Tortorella: You mean in the regular season?

Brooks: That's what I'm asking. You said you never think your backs are against the wall. Are you just talking about playoffs or any time?

Tortorella: Well, we're in playoffs right now. You're asking me questions to try and box me into language.

Brooks: No, I'm not.

Tortorella: Yes, you do.

Brooks: No, I'm not. I'm asking you do you think your backs are against the wall. You said, "I never think our backs are against the wall." I said, "In regular season or playoffs?" So you're only talking about playoffs.

Tortorella: I'm talking about a series of playoffs. Why are we even going back to regular season? Because it's logistics with you. You try to use my words . . .

Brooks: No. You talked about the regular season just now.

Tortorella: You try to use my words, Brooksie. You try to use my words and box me into a corner all the time.

Brooks: I asked you a question and I'm just trying to get an answer.

Tortorella: Can I get another question? I went in here in a pretty good mood today too.

Brooks: So did I.

Tortorella: Well you obviously f***ed that up, didn't you?

Brooks: No. You did.

•  •  •

Even though purists don't like it, the shootout is here to stay. And since that's the case, perhaps it is time to give it a closer look – maybe even do some tinkering.

There's no doubt that the concept was instituted to appease fans in the United States. A string of NHL surveys revealed Americans' overwhelming opposition to having games end in a tie.

That left the league with the option of unlimited overtime or a shootout, and given the extreme emphasis on defence that has led to so many low-scoring games, unlimited overtime could very well become unending overtime.

The league anticipated a tough time earning acceptance for shootouts in Canada, but their fears proved to be unfounded. Shootouts are extremely popular in Canada, and are even more so in the United States, where those few fans in attendance frequently stand up during the overtime in excited anticipation of a shootout.

There were some early problems with the shootout and a quick rule modification had to be introduced to allow the use of video replays. Other than that, the shootouts proceeded smoothly. But more and more, players are trying innovations that are, at best, on the edge of the rules.

The Minnesota Wild's Pierre-Marc Bouchard was the first to roar in on the goalie, do a 180-degree turn at the edge of the crease, and backhand the puck into the net. Now, we see that move – or a variation on it – probably once a shootout.

But is the puck always moving toward the net as

penalty shot rules require? It's a close call. Very close.

When the shooter is that close to the crease, is he interfering with the goalie? Granted, the goalie has no territorial rights outside his crease, but in a penalty-shot situation, isn't it unreasonable to expect him to be deprived of a chance to move towards the shooter?

Part of the problem the league faces is that it doesn't want to limit the creativity of the shooters. Sometimes those dazzling shootout goals are the highlight of the evening.

The shooters do what the fans want to see, but the fact remains that it's borderline illegal. That's why the rule needs some tinkering.

The rule-makers should find a way to allow limited backward movement of the puck. Every time it's successful, the victimized team complains, and the focus is moved away from the creativity that was involved.

Nobody wants to see the skater going around in circles until he's ready to shoot, but a move like the one Bouchard introduced is so entertaining that it has to be allowed.

And it's only a matter of time until a forward decides to flip the puck up onto the blade of his stick, carry it that way, and shoot it lacrosse-style into the net.

Lots of today's players can make that move with ease, and at the moment, there's nothing in the rules to prevent someone using it in a shootout. The only reason that no one has done so yet is the uncertainty. Every shooter believes he can beat the goalie, so he doesn't want to take a chance with an innovation that has no precedent and might be ruled illegal.

While they're holding their think-tank, the rule-makers might want to consider another option or two. Perhaps, to allow defencemen to become more frequent participants, a team might be allowed the option of taking one static shot, much like a penalty shot in soccer.

The puck is placed on the ice and the defenceman skates up and gets one whack. But the hash marks would be too close to the goal and the blue line too far away. So the league's hockey people would need to work out the ideal spot for puck placement and then see if the league's lawyers would allow it.

Perhaps another rule could require the goalie to keep one foot on the goal line until the shooter picks up the puck at centre ice. That's the rule in international hockey and something that Boston Bruins goalie Tim Thomas does out of habit.

Or perhaps, since the shootout is so popular, there should be five shooters.

Whatever variations the league wants to impose, the shootout will remain popular. It just needs a little fine tuning.

•  •  •

Amidst all the clamour about getting the NHL to return to Winnipeg, little mention was made of the weather.

I almost froze to death there one night. The Jets had played on a Sunday, and I made arrangements to meet the referee at a bar that wasn't too far from the hotel. The bar we usually frequented was closed. He had gone to the designated establishment after the game, but I had to go back to the hotel first.

With it being Sunday, there were no cabs available when I left the hotel. The streets were deserted. I decided to walk. Not a good idea. After a few blocks, I was seriously cold. I kept looking for cruising cabs. There weren't any. I kept looking for open stores or fast-food outlets or coffee shops so I could duck in and warm up, but it was a winter Sunday night in Winnipeg and everything was closed.

I was as chilled as I've ever been in my life and nearly blue by the time I got to the bar.

It is an indisputable fact that of all the cities in the world with a population in excess of 600,000, Winnipeg is the coldest.

Charlie Simmer of the Los Angeles Kings' famous Triple Crown Line once said, "The best thing about Winnipeg is the airport. You always know you can get out of town." The city does have its good points, but its weather isn't one of them.

Randy Carlyle, who played for the Jets for years and is now the coach of the Anaheim Ducks, once said, "I wouldn't want to say Winnipeg is cold, but the athlete of the year was an ice fisherman."

• • •

In 2005, the NHL instituted a rule that prevents a team that has iced the puck from changing personnel prior to the ensuing faceoff.

The reasoning behind the rule change was that it would increase scoring because a team wouldn't be able to relieve pressure simply by slamming the puck down the ice and sending out fresh troops.

After all, a tired team is more likely to surrender a goal than a fresh one. Over the years, the concept has proved to be sound.

But why stop there? Sometimes, if a player has lost or broken his stick, his team will ice the puck despite the disadvantage of doing so. They consider icing to be a better option than effectively playing short-handed because one of their players has no stick, so if a team does that, why doesn't the league keep that original premise in mind?

If one of your players is without a stick when you ice the puck, then one of your players should be without a stick during the ensuing faceoff. It doesn't have to be the same player because it's routine for a forward to give his stick to a defenceman under such circumstances. But why should a team be rewarded – or allowed to escape a dangerous situation – when it commits an infraction?

•  •  •

There are two major problems with sports talk shows: (1) callers who don't know what they're talking about and (2) hosts who don't know what they're talking about.

Neither is in short supply, and as a result, a frequent assertion on these shows is that the NHL would be much better off if it got rid of ten teams.

The hosts and callers invariably agree that as a result of the downsizing, the league would be more financially stable, the standard of play would increase dramatically, and the league's image would improve.

Nothing could be further from the truth.

Start with the image. What could be more disastrous to the image of a "big league" than to turn itself into a small league? It sends the message that a full third of the league was unable to be successful. It says that in ten cities, hockey couldn't find enough fans to be a viable proposition. It says that a third of the people who have been paid as big-leaguers were in fact minor-leaguers. It says that the NHL is now admitting that a third of the franchises it has presented as major league were in fact no such thing. They weren't even worthy of continued existence.

The argument that a smaller league would be a positive development from a financial point of view is similarly unfounded. How could a twenty-team league generate as much money as a thirty-team league? It's easy to say that the ten least-supported teams would be axed, thereby creating financial stability, but the league keeps finding owners to take over struggling franchises.

If an owner runs into financial trouble and has to sell his team, that doesn't affect the financial well-being of the league as a whole. It still has thirty owners, even if one of them is new on the scene.

What would shrinkage do to revenues from network television? The people who support downsizing invariably agree that all these unwanted teams are in the United States. So now we'd have a league that operates in only thirteen U.S. markets – counting the New Jersey Devils and New York Rangers as one market and assuming the woeful New York Islanders would be one of the casualties.

The fewer the markets, the less the league can command for its television rights. The reason that the NHL expanded in the first place was to give itself access to U.S. networks and not have any black holes on the map – areas where no team was located.

The concept has never been as successful as the league had hoped, but that has been due to the ineptitude of NHL leadership rather than a flaw in the logic.

Given the current media explosion – especially in the area of sports – limiting the number of U.S. markets to thirteen would be sheer lunacy.

And where would the money come from to buy these teams? Or is it to be assumed that the owners of the ten unwanted teams would simply shut their doors and take a loss? There's no chance of that happening.

The price of an NHL franchise these days is in the $200 million range. Ten teams would therefore be worth $2 billion. So if we get this right, the people who support a downsizing think that in order to help its financial stability, the league should spend $2 billion and have no asset left to show for its money. That's not the best economic strategy I've ever heard.

Where the hosts and their callers really show their lack of vision is in their insistence that a smaller league would create a better on-ice spectacle.

Their theory is that by getting rid of a third of the teams, the league would get rid of a third of its players and that the ones who would remain would dazzle us with their talent.

The reality is quite the opposite. In hockey, as in most team sports, defence wins. The players who would be discarded would therefore be the ones who are weakest defensively.

If a third of the players were cut loose, the ones remaining would be the ones who can best shut down the stars – the guys Alexander Ovechkin can't skate around, the goalies Sidney Crosby has trouble beating, and so on.

Goals would therefore become so rare that we'd get soccer scores every night. As a result, each goal would become more important, and coaches would stress defence even more than they did in the thirty-team league.

How would this be an improved spectacle?

It also seems to assume that either there are no good players on the disbanded teams or that these players would get divided up equally and sprinkled around the league, pushing the not-so-good players on the surviving teams out of jobs and thus raising the calibre of play across the board.

The reality is that the league would stage a dispersal draft, and the teams that draft well and scout well would do better than teams that don't. Since the teams that draft and scout well are invariably among the league's elite, it stands to reason that a dispersal draft would help the strong get stronger and make the weak teams weaker.

This is good for the league?

In Anaheim, Tampa Bay, Carolina, and Dallas, the teams have been well supported when they provided a winning team. Each of those franchises won a Stanley Cup.

When the Florida Panthers and Los Angeles Kings went to the Stanley Cup finals, local excitement was just as great as it would have been under similar circumstances in any northern city.

The viability of a team is not a matter of geographical location. It's a matter of on-ice success. The same principle applies in every other major sport. Fans will come out if the local team is winning. They'll stay home if it isn't.

Eliminating a number of Sun Belt teams might seem like a good idea on the surface, but the closer you look at it, the less attractive it becomes.

●   ●   ●

Boston Bruins goalie Tim Thomas is like a character straight out of a feel-good movie. During his career, he bounced all over the hockey world before becoming an unlikely starter and then an even less likely 2009 Vezina Trophy winner.

Except for a four-game stint in 2002–03, he didn't hit the NHL until he was thirty-one, not the normal career route, to say the least.

Thomas's itinerant past is responsible for a characteristic move that he displays every time he goes into a shootout.

He stands hunched over with one foot back, not unlike a long-distance runner awaiting the starter's gun. Then, as soon as the shooter collects the puck at centre ice, Thomas pushes off and makes a move towards him.

There's a reason for it. "In Europe you can't take your foot off the goal line until the guy touches the puck for the shootout," explained Thomas, "so it was a habit I got into when I played in Sweden. That's why my left foot is on the goal line. If I started with two feet on the goal line, I'd be too far in the net."

•  •  •

In a game in March 2011, Montreal Canadiens defenceman Hal Gill scored his first goal in a year. Exactly a year. "I'm on fire," he explained to the media.

•  •  •

Before I was bounced from *Hockey Night in Canada* for writing *Why the Leafs Suck*, I used to enjoy the verbal sparring I did with Mike Milbury.

Even though we used to yap at each other – on and off camera – neither of us took offence. In fact, we both enjoyed it.

One of the reasons I like Milbury is that he's always forthright. Typical of this was an instance in March 2011, when he was on the "Hotstove" discussing a hit by Montreal's Tomas Plekanec on Boston's Nathan Horton.

The game had taken place earlier in the week. Plekanec was trying to get past Horton, but as he was rubbed out along the boards, he twisted and fell. In doing so, he "coincidentally" whacked Horton across the face with his stick. Horton was cut and had to leave the game.

In games involving the Bruins, Mike Murphy looked into any matters that required supplementary discipline, not the usual NHL disciplinarian at that time, Colin Campbell.

Gregory Campbell, Colin's son, plays for the Bruins. Murphy decided that no suspension was warranted

"You can't tell me that that was not an intentional hit right there," said Milbury after watching Plekanec whack Horton. "I know Mike Murphy wasn't that type of player, so he probably didn't look at it that way. I *was* that type of player and I can tell you . . . that's a five-minute major and a suspension right there."

Milbury was right when he said he was that type of player. It brought to mind an incident when, as a player, he slashed Philadelphia's Rick MacLeish across the face. He was given a penalty for high-sticking, which he vigorously disputed on the grounds that MacLeish, who wasn't

very big to begin with, was skating hunched over. "My
stick wasn't high," insisted Milbury.

"Well, if you want, I can call it slashing instead," said
the referee, "and that carries an automatic $200 fine."

"I'll take the high-sticking," said Milbury.

•   •   •

Today, Brendan Shanahan works for the National Hockey
League. It's his job to mete out discipline and act as a con-
sultant on safety issues.

I always liked Shanahan, both on and off the ice. He
was an excellent, rugged player. He rarely fought, but when
he did, the other guy invariably came away bleeding.

Off the ice, he was always concerned about the direction of the game, and we often chatted about the issues
after morning skates during his years with the Detroit
Red Wings.

The Wings' dressing room wasn't known for its social
atmosphere. The prevailing attitude – naturally enough
encouraged by Scott Bowman – was more along the lines
of "Do what you need to do and get out of here." But
Shanahan, always a free spirit, never seemed to care too
much. If he wanted to chat about aspects of the game that
didn't directly affect the Wings, he would do so, whether
Bowman liked it or not.

Even in his earlier days, playing for the St. Louis
Blues, he had exhibited a concern for the game. In fact, he

was the National Hockey League Players' Association representative for the Blues and in that capacity attended a meeting between NHL executives and NHLPA player reps.

At the time, the Blues were a free-spending team with one of the highest payrolls in the league, and Jeremy Roenick, who was the player rep of the Chicago Blackhawks, made the point that he liked the way the Blues did business. Yes, they spent big money, Roenick said, but they also sold out every game. What was wrong with that?

Gary Bettman's response was that despite their free-spending ways, the Blues were eliminated in the first round of the previous year's playoffs.

Shortly afterwards, Shanahan took the floor. He said that he had been thinking about Bettman's comments and that he just happened to be very proud of the Blues. Furthermore, he said to Bettman, "From now on, when you're talking about my team, you had better take that smirk off your face."

There were no further references to the Blues' shortcomings.

# CHAPTER FIFTEEN

*Memories do not decay at a uniform atomic rate. Happiness
has the shortest half-life, a quick fade to oblivion or nos-
talgia. But shame, guilt, anger, remorse; these are heavier
isotopes, remaining toxic for a lifetime, even generations.*

Ronald Wright, *Henderson's Spear*

**When you're a full-time hockey columnist,** no
aspect of the job is really unpleasant. Like every vocation, it
has some drawbacks. But for the most part, writing hockey
columns ranks among the better ways to earn a living.

And of all the things a hockey writer does, covering an
international tournament is probably the best.

Usually, from the time the tournament's training
camp opens until the final buzzer goes and the trophy is
awarded, you work seven days a week.

But that's no real hardship. Most of the time, the toughest part of writing columns is coming up with the ideas.

I was at a paper once where they hired a columnist
who was a total failure. He indulged in ridiculous flights
of fancy. He made suggestions that no serious hockey fan

could ever accept. He proposed ideas that were impossible to implement. He wrote morning columns on the day of an important game so that he wouldn't have to face the pressures of deadline.

I abused the sports editor for hiring this guy and was told that there had been an extensive tryout. Prior to his hiring, the guy had written ten columns and they had all been good. "Anybody can write ten columns," I said. "Try writing four or five a week, every week for the rest of your life." The fact that the guy had written ten good columns didn't matter. That was all he had in him.

But writing columns at an international tournament – even seven days a week – is never a problem. The stories are all there unfolding in front of you. It's just a matter of making sure they get into the paper.

And of all the days of an international tournament, perhaps the best is the first day of training camp.

There is always a wonderful ambience. It's a mixture of a number of factors – anticipation, camaraderie, optimism, exuberance, and pride being among them. Perhaps the feeling should have passed long ago, but it never did. Every time a couple of dozen of our best players get together in a hockey rink, there is the inescapable sense that we have found the essence of Canada.

For many of those tournaments, the summer sun would be blazing outside, the country would be facing economic problems, and violence would be flaring in the world's hot spots. But in the cement bowels of a chilly, otherwise deserted hockey rink, true Canadian euphoria was on display.

Another tournament would be about to start. Another chance to show that in the only activity that is truly Canadian and unites the country, we are still best.

The rest of the world doesn't care much. Often, most of the world doesn't even know the tournament is taking place. But that's not the point.

An international tournament, whether it's the Olympics, the Canada Cup, or the World Cup, matters to Canadians. It's one more manifestation of that ritualistic torment that we like to force upon ourselves at regular intervals.

Win and all is well. Lose and we'll beat ourselves up for years until the next opportunity rolls around.

If it appears that Canada might not emerge on top, there is no limit to the abuse and scorn that is heaped upon the players. Remember the shaky start to the 2002 Olympic tournament and the vicious, acrimonious – often personal – attacks to which the team was subjected?

But when those players were winning the gold medal ten days later, all was forgiven. Now they were national heroes, the stuff of which legends are made.

At various times, depending upon the proximity of the next negotiations for a collective bargaining agreement, a lot of them are criticized as lazy, overpaid, greedy bums. But when these players get the call to play for Team Canada, they come. No hesitation. No conditions. No convenient injuries.

In some other countries, the players dread the telephone call asking them to participate. Our players sit by
the phone waiting for it, and feel acute disappointment if
it doesn't come.

They know what they're letting themselves in for.
They know that there are only two possible outcomes –
one is to win, the other is to be vilified.

But they don't back down. They don't beg off. They
come to wear the Team Canada sweater proudly, totally
determined to perpetuate the hockey heritage that has
been handed down to them.

As the tournament unfolds, there are invariably some
dark moments. There are always some controversies and
some concerns.

But opening day is the dawning of a new challenge,
and radiating from it is the optimism that always surfaces
whenever Canada sends its finest to play hockey.

How can you not love your job on a day like that?

•  •  •

You don't hear much criticism of the salary cap from
people in the National Hockey League. It's not that they
like it. They know that it's an example of the Big Lie.
Keep insisting that it's true often enough, and people will
come to believe it.

But open debate is not encouraged in the NHL. In fact,
the reason the salary cap is not criticized publicly is that any

person who does so quickly receives a rocket from the NHL head office, probably even from Gary Bettman himself.

In 2008, when he was the general manager of the Vancouver Canucks, Dave Nonis, now an assistant general manager of the Toronto Maple Leafs, experienced a brief flash of honesty.

Speaking at a chamber of commerce meeting, he called the free-agency system "a joke."

The ramifications were clear. If free agency is a joke, then the collective bargaining agreement (CBA), which codifies free agency, is also a joke. Therefore, by extension, the NHL executives who negotiated it are a joke.

If there's one thing that Bettman is consistent about, it is his insistence that you don't criticize your product. Nonis did indeed receive a rocket and never broached the matter again.

But on that one night, he told the truth. "You are going to see movement among players every single year," he said.

That's exactly what the people who refuse to accept the Big Lie have been saying ever since the lockout. The CBA creates churn. Players will come and go without any sense of loyalty.

What Nonis didn't seem to grasp is that this is exactly what the league wants.

When you've got thirty teams in your league, you don't want dynasties. You don't want one team being dominant for four or five years. For every team that's at the top for a long period, there's a team that's a cellar-dweller for the same period.

You want every team to have its brief Icarus-like moment, fluttering hopefully up towards the sun before it comes crashing down in flames.

Your commitment is not to great hockey, it's to making cash. The theory is that this recurrent optimism will keep fans coming back.

The reason that it's a Big Lie is that when Bettman shut down the league for a year, he insisted that he was "doing it for the fans."

He was going to keep ticket prices down. He was going to keep salaries down. He was going to make sure that small-market teams could compete.

In every market, ticket prices have gone up. New forms of separating fans from even more of their money – such as "premium tickets," the concept of charging more for high-profile teams – have also been introduced.

Salaries aren't down. They're where they were before the lockout, and they're trending higher every year.

The small-market teams can compete only if they spend like big-market teams. The simple fact of the matter is that teams in the bottom third of the payroll list have won only three playoff rounds since the lockout.

The NHL teams decided they wanted this salary cap system. They passed it off to the public as a means to save the small franchises when in reality it was nothing more than a scheme to make the owners richer.

Because of the stability of a cap, franchise prices are higher. Owners can sell their teams for more money.

And when the cap appeared, teams like Toronto, New York, and Detroit were able to spend a lot less on players, using the excuse of a salary cap, without any appreciable change in the calibre of team they put on the ice. The Wings remained strong, the Leafs remained weak, and the Rangers wavered in the middle.

But you won't hear any of these criticisms from anyone in the NHL. The head office doesn't allow it.

•   •   •

One last point regarding the merits of a salary cap. It was a system that, according to no less an authority than Gary B. Bettman, commissioner of the National Hockey League, had to be instituted to save the small-market teams and create a level playing field.

But that was what he said in 2004.

Here's what that same Gary B. Bettman had to say on the matter on November 10, 1999, speaking to the Sports Values and Finance Seminar in New York: "There's absolutely no correlation between how a team does competitively and its payroll. There is no correlation.

"The coefficient is down less than 50 per cent.

"It's like flipping a coin and anecdotally, those of you who are from New York, the last three years, the Rangers have had the highest payroll in the league. They didn't make the playoffs the last two years, and this year, people are already starting to scratch their heads. The Edmonton Oilers, Buffalo Sabres, Ottawa Senators have all been competitive with below-average payrolls. There is no correlation in this sport between how much you spend and how well your team performs."

•  •  •

When hockey people get together for a tournament, one bar usually emerges as the unofficial watering hole.

During one of the world junior tournaments, a large group of hockey people were sitting around one such venue on an off night, trying to discuss the state of the world.

The place was fairly crowded, and the only table we could get was near the stage, where a local rock group was making conversation difficult.

An NHL scout, whom I probably shouldn't name, shouted over at the band when they took a break. He told the three guys that he liked their music and they thanked him for his support. "How much are they paying you guys?" he asked.

"Two hundred bucks," was the response.

"I'll pay you three hundred to go home," he said. They didn't accept the offer. No one really expected they would. But isn't that something you've often wanted to do?

•  •  •

Babe Pratt was one of the great players of the six-team era, a stalwart with the Toronto Maple Leafs when they were one of the league's elite teams.

After he retired, he moved out to Vancouver, and in the early days of the Canucks, he could always be found at the rink. He'd be there for the morning skates, and he'd be in the press room before the game. He was a jovial fellow, always ready to tell a hockey story to anyone who would listen.

But late in the seventies, his health started to decline.

I ran into him in Vancouver and asked him how he was doing. "Well, let's put it this way," he said. "I told my wife not to buy me any green bananas."

• • •

It was a quiet afternoon during one of the World Cup tournaments when Tony Gallagher of the Vancouver *Province* pestered me to go to the hotel's exercise room and use some of the equipment.

While I often rode an exercise bike at home, I had it situated next to a desk so I could play computer games while I was pedalling and therefore hardly noticed that I was getting some exercise.

But I hate hotel exercise rooms, where the only diversion is CNN or CBC Newsworld, depending on which country you're in. Neither one does much to take your mind off the rigours of the exercise.

Anyway, just to get Gallagher off my case, I went to the exercise room with him. For some reason, it was fairly crowded, and we got the last two bikes.

Team Sweden was staying in the same hotel, and we hadn't been on the bikes long when Danny Alfredsson of the Ottawa Senators came in. He looked at the line of bikes, saw they were all full, and came over to us shaking his head. "I never thought I'd see the day when I couldn't get an exercise bike because the media were on them," he said.

"Good point, Danny," I said, climbing down. "Take this one."

It's always important to maintain good relationships with the players.

•  •  •

During his tenure as captain of the Detroit Red Wings, Steve Yzerman hung the nickname of "The Mule" on Johan Franzen. When asked for an explanation, Yzerman said that he chose the name because Franzen always "carried the load."

Right. And it had nothing to do with the fact that on the Wings' road trips to Florida, no one from Cape Canaveral is likely to ask Franzen to drop in for a day and double-check their calculations.

In 2010, for instance, Wings goaltender Chris Osgood was injured and out of action for ten days. When he came back, the media were wandering through the Detroit dressing room looking for pre-game stories and asked Franzen how he felt about Osgood's return.

Suddenly, Franzen looked more like a deer caught in the headlights than a mule. He frantically whispered a question to the teammate next to him. The teammate nodded. "Yeah, he's been gone ten days," he said.

The Wings scouted Franzen in Sweden – after he came back from a one-year suspension for knocking down a referee – and as part of the process, talked to his coach about him.

"He's a great player," said his Swedish coach, "but you'll have to look after him. He brings a suitcase to the rink every day because so far, he hasn't been able to figure out how the schedule works, so he always shows up with a suitcase just in case we're going on the road."

•  •  •

During the 2010–11 season, Montreal Canadiens defence-man Jaroslav Spacek suffered a knee injury that required surgery. He missed twenty-three games, and when he was due to return, he was chatting with the media and said that after the surgery, he had realized right away that the operation had been a success.

He was asked how he knew that.

"Because I woke up with two knees and no big boobs," he said.

•  •  •

Most of the time, the much-travelled coach Roger Neilson tended to be fairly serious, especially where hockey was concerned. But he had a wry sense of humour that emerged every so often.

On one occasion, the NHL had handed down a ruling that went against one of his players and Neilson was asked for his reaction.

He said that he wasn't pleased and that he felt the reasoning behind the judgment was flawed.

He was then asked how he thought the NHL had arrived at its decision. "There are two things you don't want to know in life," said Neilson. "One is what goes into hot dogs and the other is what goes on in the minds of people in the NHL head office."

•  •  •

The relationship between the different segments of the hockey media has changed radically over the years.

When I began covering hockey in 1973, the media had three distinct subgroups. One consisted of the announcers – the guys who called the play-by-play and did the colour on radio and television. Another was the newspaper faction, the beat writers and the columnists who followed the team on a day-by-day basis.

There was mutual respect between these two groups.

Both travelled with the team. Both had contacts through-out the league, and both were known by name to the fans.

The third group was made up of radio people who were really nothing more than microphone pointers. They covered the team only when it was at home and rarely asked questions other than the most inane: "Were you happy with your hat trick last game?"

They would barge into an ongoing interview, aim their microphone in the general direction of the player, and start recording. Their pay was negligible compared to the other two groups, and although it might be a stretch to say they were held in contempt by the other two groups, they certainly weren't highly regarded.

The print guys felt, with considerable justification, that they were the ones who set the agenda.

The announcers were team employees. They would do what they were told.

Radio guys were just leeches. It was the print guys who started the move to bench a player, fire a coach, or make a trade. They were the ones who broke the stories and followed them up. The radio guys just showed up later and tried to get a reaction.

But as newspapers started to decline with the rise of the internet, both in readership and in relevance, all those standards changed. Today, the TV corps comprises much more than announcers. The top-notch story breakers don't work for newspapers any more. They're either on TV, like Bob McKenzie, Darren Dreger, and a few others, or they're on the internet, like Pierre LeBrun and Scott Burnside.

The top analysts aren't writing newspaper columns either. They're part of the many TV panels – on Sportsnet and TSN in Canada, on NBC and Versus in the United States.

In my younger days, I'd have kids come up to me asking about developments in the game. That doesn't happen to newspaper people any more. Kids don't read newspapers.

And radio people? Well, for the most part, they're still the bottom of the barrel.

They're biased and proud of it. That's why the continent is full of stations calling themselves The Fan or The Team. I don't know of any called The Truth.

When they do talk to someone in the real media, they invariably end the interview with "Enjoy the game tonight."

I always wanted to say, "Enjoy the game? I'm going to work! I'm writing two or three columns during and after that game, and I'm watching for nuances that can be discussed or mistakes that determined the outcome. It's mentally demanding and it's done under strict time constraints. Do you think I'm sitting up there eating hot dogs and cheering for the home team?"

I can't listen to call-in radio any more. It's too full of people who have no idea what they're talking about, reinforcing each other's unfounded opinions. Then if someone does try to set them straight, they say, "Oh, he's just a puckhead."

Sad though it may be to an old veteran of the newspaper era, the fact of today's life is this: No matter how things used to be, if you want to know what's really going on in hockey today, watch television or surf the internet. Forget the newspapers and the radio stations.

# ACKNOWLEDGEMENTS

A book like this can't be written without a lot of assistance.

Pierre Lebrun has been a good friend for a long time now and is always supportive and helpful, setting me on the right track and offering useful suggestions. He has also offered a few suggestions that would be painful if I tried them, but that's what friends do now and then. I can't think of a time when I haven't enjoyed his company.

Lucie Leduc kept my spirits up and occasionally boosted my ego – not that it often needs a lot of help – but on those rare occasions when it did, she was there.

As is the case every time I write a book, Gail MacDonald and Dave Carter offered insights and encouragement.

Marian Strachan gave the raw manuscript her usual meticulous (some would say pedantic) examination. Being pedantic is not a bad thing for an editor.

Roy MacGregor and Wayne Gretzky once again continued to lavish the kindness that they have provided over the years.

On the business side, Brian Wood got the project rolling and provided the odd prod to those who needed them – including me.

A lot of people are quoted in this book and I thank them for their co-operation. No one refused to talk to me. Of course, I didn't call Brian Burke.

But it was the players of the National Hockey League who, as always, made the greatest contribution. Being in their company for more than three decades has been a wonderful experience.

And, as I have come to discover from writing books, there will probably be errors. If so, don't blame any of these people. The fault is mine.